Battleground Europe
WALKING THE SALIENT

Other guides in the Battleground Europe Series:

Walking the Salient *by* Paul Reed
Ypres - Sanctuary Wood and Hooge *by* Nigel Cave
Ypres - Hill 60 *by* Nigel Cave
Ypres - Messines Ridge *by* Peter Oldham

Walking the Somme *by* Paul Reed
Somme - Gommecourt *by* Nigel Cave
Somme - Serre *by* Jack Horsfall & Nigel Cave
Somme - Beaumont Hamel *by* Nigel Cave
Somme - Thiepval *by* Michael Stedman
Somme - La Boisselle *by* Michael Stedman
Somme - Fricourt *by* Michael Stedman
Somme - Carnoy-Montauban *by* Graham Maddocks
Somme - Pozieres *by* Graham Keech
Somme - Courcelette *by* Paul Reed
Somme - Boom Ravine *by* Trevor Pidgeon

Arras - Vimy Ridge *by* Nigel Cave
Arras - Bullecourt *by* Graham Keech

Hindenburg Line *by* Peter Oldham
Epehy *by* Bill Mitchenson
Riqueval *by* Bill Mitchenson

Boer War - The Relief of Ladysmith, Colenso, Spion Kop *by* Lewis Childs

Accrington Pals Trail *by* WilliamTurner

Poets at War: Wilfred Owen *by* Helen McPhail and Philip Guest

Gallipoli *by* Nigel Steel

Battleground Europe Series guides in preparation:
Ypres - Polygon Wood *by* Nigel Cave
La Basseé - Givenchy *by* Michael Orr
La Basseé - Neuve Chapelle 1915 *by* Geoff Bridger
Walking Arras *by* Paul Reed
Arras - Monchy le Preux *by* Colin Fox
Somme - Following the Ancre *by* Michael Stedman
Somme - High Wood *by* Terry Carter
Somme - Advance to Victory 1918 *by* Michael Stedman
Somme - Ginchy *by* Michael Stedman
Somme - Combles *by* Paul Reed
Somme - Beaucourt *by* Michael Renshaw

Walking Verdun *by* Paul Reed

Poets at War: Edmund Blunden *by* Helen McPhail and Philip Guest

Boer War - The Siege of Ladysmith *by* Lewis Childs
Isandhlwana *by* Ian Knight and Ian Castle
Rorkes Drift *by* Ian Knight and Ian Castle

With the continued expansion of the Battleground series a Battleground Europe Club has been formed to benefit the reader. The purpose of the Club is to keep members informed of new titles and key developments by way of a quarterly newsletter, and to offer many other reader-benefits. Membership is free and by registering an interest you can help us predict print runs and thus maintain prices at their present levels. Please call the office 01226 734555, or send your name and address along with a request for more information to:

Battleground Europe Club
Pen & Sword Books Ltd, 47 Church Street, Barnsley, South Yorkshire S70 2AS

Battleground Europe

WALKING THE SALIENT

A Walkers Guide to the Ypres Salient

PAUL REED

Series editor
Nigel Cave

LEO COOPER

Dedicated to Edmund and Poppy

First published in 1999 by
LEO COOPER
an imprint of
Pen Sword Books Limited
47 Church Street, Barnsley, South Yorkshire S70 2AS

Copyright © Paul Reed

ISBN 0 85052 617 5

A CIP catalogue of this book is available
from the British Library

Printed by Redwood Books Limited
Trowbridge, Wiltshire

*For up-to-date information on other titles produced under the Leo Cooper imprint,
please telephone or write to:*
Pen & Sword Books Ltd, FREEPOST, 47 Church Street
Barnsley, South Yorkshire S70 2AS
Telephone 01226 734222

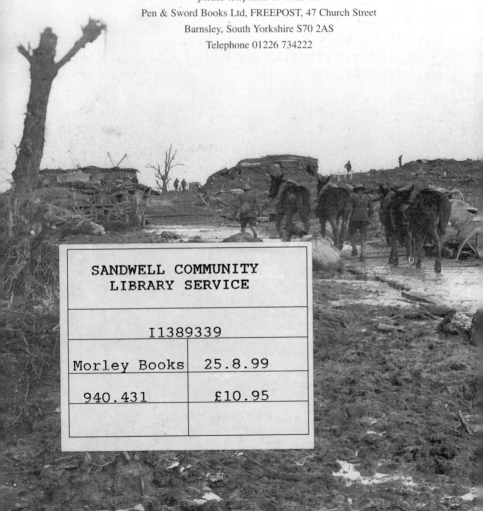

CONTENTS

PREFACE

It seemed that for most of my life all roads led to Ypres. As I grew up the names of Plugstreet Wood, Wipers and Passchendaele were not unknown to me. I was told of games of football in No Man's Land at Christmas 1914; of an uncle mortally wounded making railway sleeper roads across a moonscape of shell holes during Third Ypres; school pictures of the Cloth Hall appeared in every history text book and I recognised it as well as any building in my own town. But where was this place? What was it?

It took me many years to finally take that road to Ypres. As a fourteen year old schoolboy I sat, on a hot summer's day, in the main square outside that Cloth Hall I knew so well, when a hand touched my shoulder. The voice enquired if I was English. I was. And from where? Sussex. It was a veteran of the Great War who questioned me, a man who had fought in my own county regiment, the Royal Sussex, for over two years. He was here to find the grave of his mate, he said, last seen in March 1918. I like to think that something passed between us that day. I met him again, many years later and he was one of nearly three hundred Great War veterans I had the privilege, the honour, to know or correspond with. Some wrote me letters describing their experiences with which I could fill this book. Others wrote confessions; of mates left wounded in No Man's Land, of prisoners executed in the heat of battle – confessions of fear, pain and enjoyment. Yes, they said, many of them had enjoyed those years in the trenches. But all of them spoke in a different tone when they mentioned that place I journeyed to as an eager young teenager – Ypres.

From these men, and from the books by the likes of Campion-Vaughan, Hitchcock, Hutchison, Williamson and countless others, in my mind was built a picture of the Ypres Salient which has stayed with me all my life. Year after year I went back, each time seeing a different memorial, another cemetery, visiting another grave – or the same one as before – walking narrow lanes and fields where once were trench lines. But even in my lifetime the Salient has changed; another house was built, a factory unit thrown up or some aspect of the town meddled with. Life must go on, and it did. And it made following the men of those times more and more difficult.

The Salient is a secret I've kept for years, shared only with close friends and the dozens of veterans I knew who were there during those frightful years of death and destruction. They have all faded away now, and this book is too late for them. But just as they confessed to me, here is my confession – my Salient. And by walking it, across the Wet Flanders Plain which has taken up so much of my thoughts over countless years, you will be following in the footsteps of all those men who fought and died 'In the defence of Ypres'. Men whom Henry Williamson felt were 'lost in Ancient Sunlight', and whose ghosts cast long shadows of a summer evening at the Menin Gate as bugles call the waiting crowds to thoughtful silence.

Paul Reed
Sussex, The Somme & Flanders
August 1998

ACKNOWLEDGEMENTS

The genesis of *Walking The Salient* began a long time ago and I would like to take this opportunity to thank my former teachers at Holy Trinity School, Crawley, for taking me to the salient all those years ago: Roger Bastable and Les Coates (himself the author of two superb books on the Great War) have a lot to answer for!

Those who have walked the Salient with me include: Stephen Clarke, Colin & Lisa Gillard, Geoff Goodyear, Edmund, Tony & Joan Poucher, Terry Russell, Frank & Lou Stockdale, Pam Waugh, Andrew Whittington, and not forgetting of course the old 'Sussex Pals': Geoff Bridger, Brian Fullagar, Clive Metcalfe, Julian Sykes, and Terry Whippy.

Dozens of others helped with a multitude of tasks, among them: Commonwealth War Graves Commission office Ypres, Ron Jack who obtained a copy of Talbot Papineau's service record for me, Andy Moss, the staff of the Public Records Office, Tony Scala, Klaus Späth for the loan of several German photographs, and Tom Tulloch-Marshall.

Having organised battlefield tours to the Ypres Salient for over 3,000 people in the two years leading up to the publication of this book I would like to thank all those at Leger Travel Ltd, and the many coach operators and drivers with whom I have worked. And not forgetting the passengers – many have become good friends.

In the Salient itself the locals have often been kind and helpful. In particular I would like to mention Henk and family at the excellent Hotel Sultan who have provided many fabulous meals and a good place to rest. Albert Beke, formerly of the Ypres Salient Museum and now at In Flanders Fields, has been doing his bit to help British visitors for many years and it is always a pleasure to see him. John Woolsgrove and Christine have made 'The Shell Hole' a great meeting place for British visitors, with a bookshop in which I have spent many happy hours. Jacques Ryckebosche and the staff of Talbot House in Poperinghe are always so welcoming, and we all owe them a great debt for keeping this magical place open. Roger and family at Hooge Crater Café also have been most accommodating and lunch there with a visit to the museum is highly recommended. Charlotte Cardoen-Descamps and her family at their farm near Passchendaele have helped many pilgrims to the area, myself included, and opened up their house to our tours on numerous occasions, for which I am particularly grateful.

Unless otherwise stated, all photographs and maps are from the author's archives. As with my previous books I have tried to include a large number of previously unpublished, or rarely published, photographs which, judging by the reaction of the readership, is warmly welcome. John Giles' aerial photographs are used with the kind permission of his wife, Margery. Extracts from the works of Henry Williamson are reproduced courtesy of the H.W. Literary Estate.

Finally, my usual debt to Kieron goes without saying. She walked many of the routes with me, and helped with research and a multitude of other tasks – despite being more than seven months pregnant by the time the first draft was finished! Now we have a beautiful baby daughter, Poppy, who will no doubt be accompanying her father on many walks to come!

INTRODUCTION BY SERIES EDITOR

For many years the Salient has not been as popular a destination for the individual battlefield visitor as the Somme. This is not to say that there are not an enormous number of visitors here, certainly in relation to the situation some twenty years or so ago. School parties invariably visit the prominent sites – Tyne Cot, the trenches at Sanctuary Wood and the Last Post at the Menin Gate. Numerous veteran pilgrimages (now from the Second World War) carry out a similar act of homage under the deeply impressive arch and before the carved names that fill the walls of this evocative gate. Short guided battlefield coach tours will usually allow time for a curtailed tour of Ypres and its surrounds. But the fact remains that car tours of the battlefields in this particular sector are in the minority.

This is a great shame. It was to Ypres that I made my first tour of the battlefields, back in 1968. Then it was a rather sleepy market town and the villages even sleepier, with a quiet network of roads surrounding it. It could be that the quite significant industrial and housing developments over the last twenty-five years or so have persuaded tourers that it is too built up, that the traffic moves too fast (and there is too much of it) and that much from the Great War has been, finally, lost to the march of progress. Certainly these signs are clear for all to see – from the brash fun park at Bellewaarde, stretched over much of the fighting that took place in 1915 and 1917 around Hooge, to the industrial park to the east of the canal in Ypres itself. Roads have been cut through so as to completely alter the topography – such as that between Polygon Wood and Nonne Boschen. The piece de resistance of modern development has been the introduction of the new traffic flow system in Ypres – a nightmare for the uninitiated.

It could also be that many travellers go to the Somme because the fighting there has an interest that may be summarised in the dates 1st July 1916 to the end of November 1916. It is, in many ways, an easier battlefield to understand; and it is the first battle (and, alas, all too often the last) that many of the forebears of these tourers fought. The significant fighting on the Somme was only a matter of months in 1916, followed by some hard fights in March and April 1918 and then that August. The Salient is very different, for there were important battles here in every year of the war, and none more desperate than those of 1914 and 1917.

The battles in this part of Flanders can be confusing to follow, especially as here, almost above all, there was a great deal of to-ing and fro-ing of the line. Because of the semicircular nature of the front it is sometimes difficult to get one's bearings (difficult for us – what must it have been like for the combatants then?) and the signposting is not always of the highest quality.

Hitherto there have been guides to what became known as the 'Immortal Salient'; most recently those by John Giles and the Holts, whilst Rose Coombs' *Before Endeavours Fade* gives a very full coverage. However, this book shows how easy it is to make a large number of rewarding and illuminating walks across almost all the sectors of interest in the Salient and along Messines Ridge – walks that can be quite as quiet and contemplative as the more tranquil Somme region allows. By studying the topography it is much easier to make sense of the actions. More literature is becoming available on the battles that took place here and so it is my hope that more people will come and rediscover this special place and pay homage to those thousands – hundreds of thousands – that gave their life in that horrendous conflict.

This part of Belgium has much to offer in terms of comfortable hotels, good cuisine and beer and friendly people. There are excellent museums, notably at Hooge Chapel and Zonnebeke; there is the Last Post. But the men who fought here deserve more than a quick visit to the key visitors' sites, and I hope that this book will do much to lead them to new perspectives and understanding of the tragic events of over eighty years ago.

Nigel Cave
Ely Place, London.

USERS GUIDE

GETTING THERE: As the years progress Ypres seems to get nearer and nearer to the channel ports. It is now possible to do the journey from Calais in just over an hour following the motorway via Dunkirk, coming off at Steenvoorde and then going via Poperinghe. Those on a budget will be pleased to know this stretch of motorway is toll-free. Getting to Ypres via public transport is somewhat more difficult. There are no direct rail links from the ports or the channel tunnel, and if coming by train from France the visitor must pass via Lille and then cross the border at Comines (Komen), and take a train for Ypres from there. All these services are infrequent. With the closure of the Ypres-Roulers railway line some years ago, there are no direct trains from the Belgian ports of Zeebrugge or Ostend, but from the latter there is a

A modern aerial view of Ypres showing the Cloth Hall, St Martin's Cathedral and the Menin Gate. (John Giles)

good bus service – but be prepared for a long journey.

ACCOMMODATION: There are many hotels in Ypres, and the prices very greatly. The area does not abound with Bed & Breakfast establishments as with the Somme, and the only English person currently offering this is John Woolsgrove at 'The Shell Hole', D'Hondstraat 54-56, 8900 Ieper, Belgium. Tel/Fax: (0032) 57.20.87.58. Charlottte Cardoen-Descamps has opened another at 'Varlet Farm' near Passchendaele. Tel/Fax: (0032) 51.77.78.59. Ypres has a very good, clean campsite with excellent facilities for tents, caravans and campers. Tel: (0032) 57.21.72.82. Full details of these and others are available from the Ypres Tourist Office (see below).

EATING OUT: The main square (Grote Markt) in Ypres has a profusion of places to find food and drink of all kinds and to suit all pockets. 'Frituurs', chip shops, are everywhere – the Belgians love their chips, especially dunked in mayonnaise. Most of the villages around Ypres have a bar, often a small supermarket or other shops, and so walkers will be better served compared to Northern France.

GETTING ABOUT: Although most visitors to the battlefields come with their car or other vehicle, Ypres is served by a very good bus service which goes out to most of the villages mentioned in this book. The main bus terminus is in the Grote Markt outside the Cloth Hall, where timetables are clearly displayed. Flanders being largely flat, cycle riding is a popular pastime and many roads have their own cycle paths. Cycles of various kinds can be hired in a number of places – again ask at the Tourist Office.

TOURIST OFFICE: Ypres boasts perhaps the best tourist office anywhere on the Western Front battlefields, whose staff speak most central European languages and English fluently. There are free leaflets on most aspects of tourism in the area, and other inexpensive ones with specialist information – such as mountain bike routes, for example. Hotel bookings can be made here, taxis can be called and enquiries regarding vehicle or cycle hire are also answered. The office publishes a yearly updated list of hotels, B & Bs and camping sites which can be obtained free from: Ieper Dienst voor Toerisme, Stadhuis, Grote Markt, 8900 Ieper, Belgium. Tel: (0032) 57.20.07.24. Fax: (0032) 57.21.85.89.

COMMONWEALTH WAR GRAVES COMISSION: The head office for this part of Europe is located at 82 Elverdingestraat, Ieper. Tel: (0032) 57.20.01.18. Enquiries regarding the location of a war grave can be made here using the newly computerised records. For relatives there is no charge, but donations are always welcome.

Michelin maps overprinted with the location of cemeteries and memorials are also on sale here.

BELGIAN PLACE NAMES: Those who have visited this area will not fail to have noticed that there are variations in the spelling of places names with those found on British Great War maps. Ypres is now known as Ieper, for example. This is because Flanders is a Flemish speaking area of Belgium. In this book, unless necessary, all the names quoted are those which were commonly in use during the Great War. Doing otherwise, as several recent guidebooks have attempted, just causes confusion.

THE WALKS: The terrain around Ypres is very different to the Somme, and there are fewer cart tracks and more metalled roads. Those who have used *Walking The Somme* will therefore notice some differences here, and the ever present hand of road and building development continues to threaten areas of the Salient. However, walking the ground will still present the visitor with a new insight into the battlefields. As with my previous walking book, the walks are designed for individuals or small groups with transport which can be left and then walked back to following the designated route. However, those with a good knowledge of the area could easily adapt two or more walks to make a longer one reflecting your own interest in the battlefield. All routes are suitable for mountain bikes.

THE IRON HARVEST: Although not as noticeable as the Somme, vast numbers of shells, grenades and other munitions turn up when the farmers plough the fields around Ypres. Here they are regularly collected by the bomb squad and disposed of in a special compound in Houthulst Forest. The earth at Ypres decays metal objects into unrecognisable lumps of rust and munitions often appear harmless. Any such items should be left well alone. Safe souvenirs can be bought at most of the museums, and at 'The Shell Hole' in Ypres.

THE WESTERN FRONT ASSOCIATION: For those with more than a passing interest in the Great War, membership of the Western Front Association is essential. Founded by author John Giles in 1980, the WFA has branches all over the United Kingdom, and indeed overseas – some of which meet on a monthly basis. The annual subscription includes copies of the in-house newsletter, The Bulletin, and the glossy magazine, Stand To! Members also have access to the WFA's collection of trench maps and cheap photocopies of them are available – including many of the Ypres Salient. For further details contact:
The Western Front Association, PO BOX 1914, Reading, Berkshire, RG4 7YP.

Chapter One

YPRES TOWN WALK

STARTING POINT: **Cloth Hall, Ypres.**

DURATION: **3 hours (excluding time at In Flanders Fields museum).**

WALK SUMMARY: *A fairly short walk around picturesque Ypres following many of the places in the town associated with its occupation by British troops during the Great War. Particularly suitable for inexperienced walkers.*

Ypres has been known by many names over the centuries and now, being within the Flemish region of Belgium, is called Ieper. By the fourteenth century Ypres was the centre of the European cloth trade; the material being bought and sold in the magnificent building of the Cloth Hall, which dates from 1260. The population of the town at this time was over 40,000. Fortified by Vauban in the late 1600s, Ypres was

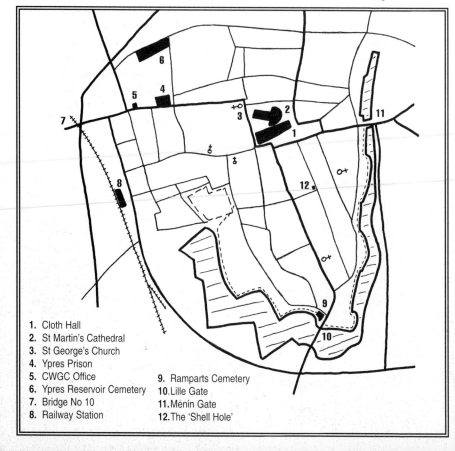

1. Cloth Hall
2. St Martin's Cathedral
3. St George's Church
4. Ypres Prison
5. CWGC Office
6. Ypres Reservoir Cemetery
7. Bridge No 10
8. Railway Station
9. Ramparts Cemetery
10. Lille Gate
11. Menin Gate
12. The 'Shell Hole'

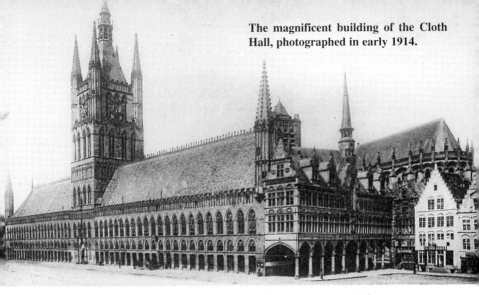

besieged on many occasions. British soldiers under the infamous Grand Old Duke of York fought in Flanders in 1793, and at the time of Waterloo the British occupied Ypres itself and its defences were improved by an officer of Engineers. By the time of the Great War the town was very much in decline and its population substantially diminished. However, in October 1914 Ypres stood in the way of the German advance on the channel ports and within a matter of a few months following the fighting here it became a symbol of sacrifice and defence against the German aggressor – and the cockpit of the British sector of the Western Front. Stories of the town filled the press as the war progressed and many people have left us their impression of it. The poet Laurence Binyon, best known for the poem, *For The Fallen*, wrote the following, simply entitled Ypres.

She was a city of patience; of proud name.
Dimmed by neglected Time; of beauty and loss;
Of acquiescence in the creeping moss.
But on a sudden fierce destruction came
Tigerishly pouncing; thunderbolt and flame
Showered on her streets, to shatter them and toss
Her ancient towers to ashes. Riven across,
She rose, dead, into never-dying fame.

White against heavens of storm, a ghost, she is known
To the world's ends. The myriads of the brave
Sleep round her. Desolately glorified,
She, moon-like, draws her own far-moving tide
Of sorrow and memory; toward her, each alone,
Glide the dark dreams that seek an English grave.

By the end of the war Ypres and its many beautiful buildings were in ruins, and a quarter of a million British and Empire soldiers – one in four of those who died in the Great War – had died in its defence. As early as 1919 veterans began to return to the battlefields where they had fought, and relatives came in search of the grave of a loved one or the place of his death if missing. As the town was slowly rebuilt, a veritable industry grew up around these pilgrimages and many ex-soldiers lived and worked in Ypres. Others stayed on to work in the military cemeteries being made more permanent by the then Imperial War Graves Commission.

Battlefield tours continued up until just before the Second World War, there being a revival of interest in the war during the 1930s – and also following the unveiling of the Menin Gate in 1927 and its moving Last Post ceremony (see below). Ypres fell after a short but decisive battle in May 1940, and four years of occupation followed. Liberated by the Polish Armoured Brigade in September 1944, the events of an even greater war put Ypres and the trenches of the Western Front into shadow for many years, and there were few visitors to the old Salient. A further revival took place in the late 1970s and early 1980s, just as the men who fought here began to 'fade away', like all old soldiers. Today the numbers who visit Ypres and its surrounding battlefields annually top 100,000 and the interest is ever growing; clearly testified to by the popularity of the *Battleground Europe* series of guide books.

The huge square of the GRANDE PLACE, or Grote Markt as it is today, was the main thoroughfare through this part of Ypres. Many battalions crossed its cobbled surfaced to go up to the trenches via the Menin Gate. On one occasion in September 1915 men of the 10th Bn West Riding Regiment were caught by shell-fire in the square on their way up to Hooge, suffering many casualties. The graves of those who died that day are buried in Ypres Reservoir Cemetery (visited later in the walk). Hugh Pollard gives a typical account of a journey into Ypres.

Entering Ypres in wartime was like entering a tomb; streets and houses were alike obliterated and rough paths cut through the ruins towards the Grande Place and the ruin of the Halles, and along where streets had once been, were the only roads. There was utter silence but for the guns and the whole air was heavy with the indescribable scent of war – a blend of chemicals, chloride of lime, and the vague plaster smell of crushed old buildings. Ypres was not a town, but a desert.[1]

The last shell to fall in the square was on 14th October 1918; two soldiers were killed by the explosion.

The CLOTH HALL has been restored to its former glory, but the work was not finished until as late as 1962. It was first struck by shells and seriously damaged in November 1914, resulting in a fire which gutted much of the upper floor. Gradually shells reduced the building to ruins, but its familiar structure became a landmark to the British soldiers who came through Ypres in the war years. Huntley Gordon records one such visit in July 1917, while serving with 112th Bde RFA.

> *Presently we reached the Square, where stands the famous Cloth Hall. I've heard of the Taj Mahal by moonlight – but for me it could never be so impressive as this ruin. The stones and masonry gleamed snowy white and the massive tower stood there, raising its jagged turrets against the dark sky like some huge iceberg. Its base emerged from a vast heap of fallen masonry that had been brought down from above, and levelled off into a sea of brick and stone rubble all around the cobbled square. There it stood, the shattered but invincible emblem of all that the Ypres Salient means – awe-inspiring and unforgetable.*[2]

Many soldiers were so inspired by the spectacle they souvenired pieces of it and took them home. Two officers of the Royal Naval Air Service were caught doing this in 1915, and as many of the townspeople of Ypres were still living in the area at this time, the subsequent Courts Martial felt the act bordered on looting. However, the two officers survived their brush with military law. Others were never caught, and hundreds of pieces of the old Cloth Hall, the Cathedral and indeed many other buildings, are preserved in the collection of the In Flanders

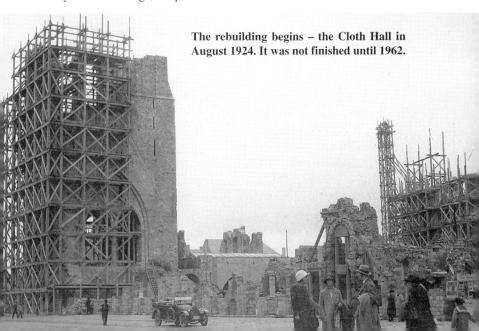

The rebuilding begins – the Cloth Hall in August 1924. It was not finished until 1962.

Fields museum; returned many years later by the men who took them.

Inside the Cloth Hall today are many of the town council offices which are not open to the public, but on the ground floor is the excellent TOURIST OFFICE (see Users Guide) which has a wealth of useful information on the local area and staff who speak fluent English. Nearby is the entrance to the IN FLANDERS FIELDS MUSEUM. The entrance is via the central archway and up a flight of stairs. This new museum, which replaced the old one in April 1998, chronicles the history of the Ypres Salient using objects, visual images, poetry and a superb 'No Man's Land' section which is one of the highlights of a visit. Computer terminals provide access to CD-ROMs which contain further, more detailed information on a variety of topics. Eventually visitors will be able to access a database of soldiers who fought and died at Ypres, being able to add their own details, of a relative for example. The exit brings you into the museum shop located next to the Tourist Office. In the shop a wide variety of souvenirs are on sale, including many books in the *Battleground Europe* series. It takes on average two hours to see the museum properly, and walkers should decide for themselves whether they do this before or after the walk; it returns here later on.

Leaving the entrance to the museum, continue under the archway into a cobbled parking area in front of ST MARTIN'S CATHEDRAL. The original St Martin's dated from the thirteenth century, although a place of worship had existed on this site since 1073. Before the war the spire was much shorter than today, although plans had been made to

St Martin's Cathedral in ruins, c.1919. The sign warned souvenir hunters that this was 'holy ground...no stone of this fabric may be taken away'.

change this. These were eventually realised in the post-war reconstruction as by 1918 the cathedral was almost completely destroyed by shelling.

The cathedral was often used by troops billeted in or passing through Ypres and a tragic episode took place here in August 1915 when the 6th Bn Duke of Cornwall's Light Infantry (DCLI) of 14th (Light) Division were in the town before moving up the line. Coming up from Vlamtinghe on 10th August, the battalion made use of the many cellars in Ypres then allocated for billeting purposes. These deep brick lined natural dugouts usually offered good protection against German shelling. On the same occasion it was discovered by a DCLI officer that the cloisters of St Martin's were still in good condition, as yet untouched by shell-fire, and C and D companies were detailed to rest there. The Battalion War Diary tells what happened two days later, on 12th August 1915.

Enemy commences to shell cloisters and Place at 6.15am. The men in the cloister thinking they were safe did not move. Enemy guns or gun fire every quarter of an hour and after a few shots got the exact range of the cloisters. The first direct hit brought down most of the W. end of cloister ceiling and buried several men. The enemy continued to fire for five hours, putting in 17-inch shells at first every quarter and later every half hour, with smaller shells and shrapnel in between. Many of the men who went to rescue their comrades were themselves buried. The warning was first conveyed to Bn HQ whereupon Major Barnett and the adjutant Lt R.C.Blagrove ran over to the cloisters to endeavour to get the men out. Both were instantly killed by the explosion of a very large shell which apparently fell in [the] open square just north of the cloisters.[3]

The remaining officers of 6th DCLI put out a warning for men to keep away from this shelled area fearing further casualties, but the non-conformist chaplain, Captain Harris, went back with four volunteers from the battalion to try and get the injured out. Harris himself was wounded on this occasion, but rescue attempts continued when soldiers from the 11th Bn King's Liverpool Regiment, the divisional pioneer battalion, arrived to assist. Some men were pulled from the rubble but casualties that morning amounted to two officers and eighteen other ranks killed, two officers and nineteen other ranks wounded. Later it was discovered that the gun which had shelled the cathedral was firing from Houthoulst Forest, over ten miles away, and had been directed by a German aeroplane which had spotted an observation post in the tower of St Martin's. The sad conclusion to this episode came after the war during the reconstruction of the cathedral when several bodies of 6th DCLI men were found in the ruins. Some accounts claim this to have been as many as forty, others more than a hundred, but graves in Ypres Reservoir Cemetery do not bear this out.

Go inside the cathedral by the door visible on the other side of the parking area. There are several memorials and commemorative windows connected with the Great War around the interior. Coming back outside and turning left follow the cathedral round to a small green with a Celtic cross set on it. This is a memorial to the men from Munster, in particular the Royal Munster Fusiliers, who fell in the Salient 1914-18. From here continue to follow the cathedral round in an anti-clockwise direction. Eventually you will come out into an area of rubble and broken statues. These are all from the original cathedral, and were so damaged that they could not be set in place again. From here continue towards the west door but join the road that runs in front and turn right, crossing another area of parking to a church with a Cross of Sacrifice on the roof and located on the corner of Elverdingestraat.

ST GEORGE'S MEMORIAL CHURCH was once symbolic of the very large English community in Ypres, which existed between the wars. The church was designed by Sir Reginald Blomfield, who had also designed the Menin Gate, and was built between 1928-29. The idea was to provide a typical English church for pilgrims to the battlefields and cemeteries. Regiments, divisions and units, as well as individual families, were invited to place memorial plaques within the church and each pew was given in memory of a soldier who died at Ypres. Today St George's is a quiet place of peace and meditation, a welcome break from the busy streets of Ypres. With its many memorials, which continue to be added to each year, it is a museum in its own right and services are held here regularly. The British settlement is much diminished, the school to the rear of the church closing after the Second World War. However, part of the site is now the branch headquarters of the local British Legion. A memorial in the entrance to the school buildings commemorates every Etonian who fell at Ypres – Eton college donated a great deal of money towards the construction of the settlement in the 1920s. The upkeep of the church is managed by the Friends of St George's, who welcome donations or offers of help.

Leaving the church turn left and continue down Elverdingestraat.

This was a busy route into Ypres and the main square during the war. Soon a turning to the right appears and opposite is the entrance to the large Ypres prison building. Stop here.

THE PRISON was one of the strongest buildings in Ypres; Rudyard Kipling remarked that it was '...a fine example of the resistance to shell-fire of thick walls if they are thick enough.' Because of this an Advanced Dressing Station (ADS) was established here in late 1915, and many other units used the rooms within, among them the Town Major of Ypres. A telephone exchange linked the prison to all the major sites between here and Poperinghe.

If you wish to visit the offices of the Commonwealth War Graves Commission, where enquiries about war graves can be made, and maps showing the location of cemeteries and memorials purchased, continue along Elverdingestraat. The office is a little further up on the right at No 82. Otherwise turn right here down Minneplein and follow the wall of the prison until a military cemetery appears on the left. Follow the road left and the entrance is seen a little further along.

YPRES RESERVOIR CEMETERY

Originally known as Ypres Prison Cemetery, as it backed onto the prison which served as an ADS, the name was changed after the war so that the relatives of the men buried here did not think their loved one had died in prison. It was by no means the only cemetery in Ypres, and there were many isolated graves and small graveyards throughout the town. Those from the western area of Ypres were brought into this cemetery after the war. Others were moved out of Ypres to cemeteries further afield, such as Bedford House and Tyne Cot.

This cemetery was started in October 1915, about the time the ADS opened, on a field that was known locally as the 'plaine d'amour' – the

Ypres Reservoir Cemetery in 1919.

field of love. It remained in use until October 1918, and a few burials were also added after the Armistice. The cemetery was used largely as a burial place for men killed in the line just outside Ypres, or for those killed in the town itself either by shell-fire or accidents. In total there are 2,248 British graves along with 151 Canadian, 142 Australian, twenty-eight New Zealand, twelve South African, six British West Indies, four Newfoundland, two Royal Guernsey Light Infantry, one Indian and one German. Seven additional burials are men whose nationality or unit is not known, and of the overall total 1,035 are unidentified. There are twelve Special Memorials.

In Plot V, Row AA are the graves of men from 6th Bn DCLI who died when the cloister of St Martin's cathedral was shelled (see above). Major C.Barnett and Lieutenant & Adjutant R.C.Blagrove, who died in the rescue attempt, are both found here. Elsewhere, Second Lieutenant Hugh Cholmeley's grave (I-D-82) is most unusual. It bears an inscription showing that he died on 7th April 1916 whilst serving with the 1st Bn Grenadier Guards on the Canal Bank sector. A second inscription commemorates his brother, Lieutenant Harry L.Cholmeley, who was killed at Beaumont-Hamel (Somme) on 1st July 1916; he has no known grave and is listed by name on the Thiepval Memorial. Not far away headstones commemorate two other brothers, one of whom was brought into this cemetery under unusual circumstances. Captain H.B.Knott (V-B-16) died of wounds with the 9th Bn Northumberland Fusiliers on 7th September 1915. His brother, Major J.L.Knott DSO (V-B-15), was killed at Fricourt on the Somme on 1st July 1916, whilst second in command of 10th Bn West Yorkshire Regiment. Although originally buried on the Somme, Major Knott's body was brought to Ypres Reservoir Cemetery after the war on the express wishes of the brothers' parents – a most rare, if not unique, occurrence.

Four gunners from the headquarters of A Battery 296th Bde RFA are buried side by side. Major F.Devonport DSO MC (I-F-39), Captain A.A.Parker (I-F-38), Lieutenant H.P.Jackson (I-F-40) and Battery Sergeant Major F.R.Heath (I-F-41) all died at Wieltje on 25th September 1917 when an 8-inch shell scored a direct hit on their battery mess. All four had long war service, and were brought back here for burial by their men: Wieltje was then under continuous shell-fire[4].

A highly decorated senior officer lies in Ypres Reservoir Cemetery, close to the Stone of Remembrance. Brigadier General F.A.Maxwell VC CSI DSO and bar (I-A-37) was mortally wounded in the Battle of the Menin Road Ridge, dying on 21st September 1917, aged forty six.

The entrance to Ypres Reservoir Cemetery in the mid-1920s.

Maxwell was an Indian Army officer of the 18th Lancers, who had won the VC on 21st March 1900 for saving the guns of a RHA battery whilst attached to Lord Robert's Horse at Korn Spruit in the Boer War. The inscription on his headstone reads, 'An ideal soldier and a very perfect gentleman. Beloved by all his men'.

Brigadier General F.A.Maxwell VC

The cemetery also contains the graves of men serving with the many support units operating in the Ypres Salient. There are gunners from Siege Batteries who had their gun sites in the town; Engineers from Field Companies, Tunnelling Companies, electrical units, road construction companies and light railways; Military Policemen, much feared and disliked, rest here – one can only contemplate their fate, although many were killed on road traffic duty, a dangerous job when shelling was heavy. It is a cemetery which reflects well the myriad of units that came to Ypres, in a quiet location with good views of the Cloth Hall and St Martin's Cathedral.

Leaving the cemetery by the main gate, turn left and continue up the street that runs alongside. Where it joins a main road (going north to Dixmude) turn left and walk down to a small roundabout, keeping to the path. During the war the famous Ypres Water Tower stood near this junction. Here turn right and again staying on the pavement follow this road until it reaches a railway line. Cross the line to a small bridge over the Comines canal.

This was known as Bridge Number Ten on British maps and was the main route into the town from the billeting areas between Ypres and Poperinghe. Just beyond where you are, at the Ypres Asylum – an ADS

'3 Knuts in Ypres': three British soldiers photographed by a local photographer in the streets of the town in 1915/16.

manned by RAMC Field Ambulances – was a notice which read 'Tin hats must be worn from here onward'. Hugh Pollard came into Ypres via this junction along,

> '...shell-pitted roads to the deep cut of the Ypres Canal, to halt awhile along the bank, which is trenched and seamed with shrapnel-proof dugouts. At intervals of a hundred yards are bridges of planks across pontoons – men are fishing and bathing in the water.'[5]

Return to Ypres by the same route, turning right at the first mini-

A soldier of the Army Service Corps photographed on the shell-damaged platform of Ypres railway station during the winter of 1914/15.

roundabout following signs for the Station down Fochlaan. The station is soon reached on the right.

Ypres railway station was on the line to Roulers and Comines, but today trains only run to Comines on the Belgian/French border and Poperinghe. It remained open for most of the war, with branch lines made off it to the many camps and dumps west of Ypres. Ammunition and supplies were also brought up here, along with tanks during Third Ypres. However, in April 1918 when the German offensive got as far as Hell Fire Corner, the station could not be used as the town was too heavily shelled. In ruins by the Armistice, it was totally rebuilt in a modern style unlikely to attract the present day visitor.

Ypres railway station in 1919.

The infantry barracks in 1914.

Outside the station, cross the main road by the traffic lights and follow Stationstraat to the junction of Templestraat and then turn right and follow the road round to where it meets De Montstraat. Once in this road stop.

To the right of this road was the famous Ypres Infantry Barracks, the strongest and safest billets in the town. A pre-war Belgian army complex, it had very thick walls and could house thousands of men at one time. At the war's end it was one of the few buildings still standing, although badly damaged. Men slept in barrack rooms designed for a fraction of that number, but parts of the place were lit by an electric generator. Men could safely light fires and cook here, although it came under increased fire in April 1918 when the front lines were so close to Ypres. Also known as 'The Esplanade' the Infantry Barracks contained a small military cemetery consisting of fourteen graves dating from April 1915 to July 1916 – ten of them from 6th Siege Battery who had their gun sites here. These were later removed to Ypres Reservoir Cemetery.

Continue along this road, taking the first turning on the right, which will take you up on to the remaining section of the Vauban Ramparts which once defended Ypres.

The Ramparts, originally dating from the 17th century, were used extensively by the British during the Great War. Casemates inside housed billets, stores and headquarters. In several places they were loop-holed for extra defence and machine-gun positions established. Observation officers used the Ramparts to look down on the battlefield immediately around the town. When the Germans got to Hell Fire Corner in April 1918 the Ramparts became part of the defence line and men of the Royal Engineers added a number of pillboxes. These may

26

The barracks in 1919: their solid walls withstood even the largest of shells.

be seen as you walk along the next section of the Ramparts leading up to the Lille Gate. A path takes you along the Ramparts at this point and eventually leads to a military cemetery.

RAMPARTS CEMETERY (LILLE GATE)

The French were the first to bury their dead on the Ramparts in 1914, during First Ypres. British burials began in February 1915 and continued until April 1918. The French crosses have long gone and now there are 153 British, fourteen New Zealand, eleven Australian, and ten Canadian graves. The cemetery register unusually records,

This is one of the smallest of the Ypres cemeteries, but in some ways the most interesting. It is the only one which commands a view of the country round; and by its position it brings together the wars of the eighteenth and twentieth centuries.

The first burials are in Rows B and C, and are from a mix of units

Old soldiers return to see the grave of a comrade in the Ramparts Cemetery, Lille Gate.

holding the Salient in early 1915 – regulars and territorials. Members of the RAMC are numerous, men from Field Ambulances which used the Ramparts. Also seen are soldiers from RE units, particularly Tunnelling Companies. The most senior officer is Major G.H.Walford (F-1) of the Suffolk Regiment, who was Brigade Major of 84th Brigade and was killed at Zonnebeke on 19th April 1915 – just prior to the gas attack of Second Ypres. This picturesque and quiet spot is often a welcome change from the busy town centre, and was a favourite of the late author, Rose Coombes. Nearby a walk along the Ramparts is named in her honour. Speculation also suggests that her ashes are scattered here.

Return to the Ramparts path and follow it across the bridge over the Lille Gate.

The Lille Gate was a major route out of Ypres, perhaps more so than the more famous Menin Gate further along the Ramparts. For most of the war years battalions could leave the town from here largely unobserved by the Germans and were therefore less likely to be shelled going to and from the trenches. Marching south they could turn off at Shrapnel Corner (visible from here) for the line at Zillebeke, or on the way to Hill 60 or The Bluff. There is a door on the Ypres side of the gate which between the wars housed a museum. During the war it contained one of the most luxurious dugouts in the Salient, built and manned by men of the Canadian Tunnelling Companies who rested here while undertaking mining operations on the Messines Ridge in 1917. It has also been claimed that General Plumer had his headquarters in this dugout during Third Ypres, but this is unlikely. What is well known is that a trench newspaper, The Wipers Times, was started here in 1916 by an officer of the 24th Division. Close to the door, on the wall of the gate, are a number of the original Imperial War Graves Commission cemetery signs – now very rare.

The street going north from the Lille Gate is Rijselsestraat (Rue de Lille during the war) and further along on the right was the site of Little Talbot House, an outpost of the more famous one in Poperinghe (see Poperinghe walk). Rev. P.B.'Tubby' Clayton, and his helpers, opened this one nearer the front line for the many men garrisoned in Ypres, but it often had to close due to shell-fire and damage. A plaque on the wall of the modern building records its former use, and can be walked to from here but it may be better to see it as a follow-up visit after the walk.

Once across the bridge continue on the path as it follows the line of the Ramparts. The moat is more visible here, but take care along the

The casemates below the Ramparts at Ypres: used as dugouts, stores and an ADS.

edge as the bricks are uneven and it is a long drop into the moat!

You are soon on the eastern edge of Ypres, and soon the spire of St Jacques church will be visible to the left. There were many dugouts in this section of the Ramparts. H.S.Clapham was here with the Honourable Artillery Company in June 1915 and recorded in his diary,

> *I am now on guard in a miniature trench on top of the ramparts of Ypres. The wall in front goes sheer down fifty feet or more into a moat, one hundred yards broad. At my back the ramparts slope upwards dotted with big trees...The sun is shining, the birds are singing but beneath all other sounds there is one deep undertone, the buzzing of innumerable flies.*
>
> *On the other side of the moat there is a brickyard, some three hundred yards long. Broken beams stick out of the piles of bricks at intervals, but there is nothing else to show that the brickyard was once a row of cottages. A dead cow lies half in the water of the moat. Spurts of flame, every now and then, disclose the position of a British battery...as I watch, a huge shell bursts in the moat, raising column of mud and water, and two others find the brickfield amid clouds of red dust. Each time a shell bursts, I duck while the debris putters among the surrounding trees.*[6]

From here Clapham could look back into the town and see what was left of the nearby St Jacques church.

> *The interior, seen from all sides through the broken walls, is a pink heap of brick and plaster. The other walls have gone, but I can see a processional cross leaning against a corner of the inner wall, and in another stands the lamp which is carried*

before the Host.

In the city the roofs which remained are stripped of tiles. Not a house seems to remain undamaged, and through the broken walls of those least damaged one can see all the household goods. Everything seems to have been abandoned...Above the town two towers still keep watch. Half of the one has gone, but two pinnacles are still intact. The other, that of the cathedral, still remains, a square mass, all its decoration gone, but its bulk untouched. For how long? Some fifty shells fell into the town last night, disturbing the rubbish and bringing down a few more walls. It is the strangest sight I have ever seen, but the worst thing about it is that buzzing undertone.[7]

Continue along the path. It will eventually bring you to the Menin Gate.

The Menin Gate was one of several breaches in the Ramparts allowing access to and from Ypres. A bridge crossed the moat here and the entrance was guarded by two huge stone lions – the symbol of Flanders. In October 1914 German cavalry entered Ypres for a brief time via this route, and the same year British troops left the town via the gate for the first time as they proceeded along the Menin Road towards the battlefront. In later years the closeness of the front lines at Hooge and Bellewaarde Ridge made it a dangerous exit from Ypres. Huntley Gordon recalled in July 1917,

For sheer concentrated shelling the Menin Gate stands alone. There is of course no gate there, merely a gap in the stone ramparts of the town, and a causeway crossing the wide moat beyond. Most of the traffic supplying the line in front of Ypres must pass through here, and the Boche takes heavy toll of it – night and day. The bridge, whether originally arched or not, is now a solid mass of stonework, supplemented, indeed cemented, by the remains of smashed vehicles and the fragmented bodies of horses and men. In fact everything that passes over it has contributed to its upkeep. During lulls in the shelling, men dash out from their shelters on the massive ramparts, and patch the holes in the road as best they can.[8]

A war-time saying was 'Tell the last man through to bolt the Menin Gate' and there can have been few soldiers who served at Ypres who did not know of or had travelled through this important landmark. It therefore seemed a most appropriate place to locate the proposed memorial to the missing of the Ypres Salient when the Imperial War

30

British dugouts by the Menin Gate, 1915

Graves Commission began to consider sites in the early 1920s. The Menin Gate was completed by July 1927, and soon after the Last Post ceremony became a regular feature each evening at 8pm – the only gap in its playing being the years of German occupation 1940-44. The memorial suffered some damage in May 1940 when it was being used as an observation post by Royal Artillery officers, to watch the advancing German Blitzkrieg as it approached Ypres. British Engineers blew the moat bridge, the resulting explosion and fragments of cobble and brick taking chunks out of the Portland stone pillars. Evidence of this is still visible today on the moat side of the archway. The Last Post ceremony is an essential part of any visit to the Salient, and no matter how many times one hears it, the tones of those bugles as they echo round the archway are as moving as the first time you attended the Menin Gate. Many people now feel moved to clap at the conclusion of the ceremony, while others might feel this a wholly inappropriate gesture.

MENIN GATE MEMORIAL

The Imperial War Graves Commission (IWGC) was founded under a Royal Charter in 1917, and as the war progressed it soon became apparent that many thousands of men would either remain missing, or be buried in unmarked graves or under a wooden cross simply marked 'unknown soldier'. The Commission therefore decided to erect a number of memorials to the missing at major points along the old Western Front, and the Menin Gate was chosen a suitable site to

The Menin Gate in 1914: the two lions – symbol of Flanders – are clearly visible.

commemorate those from the fighting at Ypres. However, the number of men who died in the Salient, and have no known grave, was so vast that the IWGC soon ran out of space on the Menin Gate when the figure reached 55,000 and an extension for a further 35,000 names was constructed at Tyne Cot. For no particular reason the cut off date between the two memorials is midnight on 15th August 1917, when the Battle of Langemarck began. The Menin Gate therefore commemorates men who died on or before that date, many of the names being soldiers who fell at First Ypres in 1914. The only exceptions are the Australians, Canadians and South Africans – all their missing from the Salient are listed on these panels.

The following commemorations are those made on the Menin Gate:

British – 40,244
Canadian – 6,983
Australian – 6,198
South African – 564
Indian – 421
West Indian – 6

The poet Siegfried Sassoon felt the Menin Gate was a 'sepulchre of crime', but Field Marshall Lord Plumer appealed to the many families of those honoured here when he said at the unveiling in July 1927, 'They are not missing – they are here'. Like other memorials to the missing, the Menin Gate recalls so many lives that it is difficult at times to come to terms with the sheer numbers of men whose names lines these walls. Among them are eight Victoria Cross winners:

Four years later: shell damage, barbed wire and sandbags.

L/Cpl	F.Fisher	13th Canadians	VC – 23.4.15	Killed – 24.4.15
CSM	F.W.Hall	8th Canadians	VC – 24.4.15	Killed – 25.4.15
2/Lt	D.G.W.Hewitt	14th Hampshires	VC – 31.7.17	Killed – 31.7.17
Lt	H.McKenzie DCM	7th Coy CMGC	VC – 30.10.17	Killed – 30.10.17
Capt	J.F.Vallentin	1st South Staffs	VC – 7.11.14	Killed – 7.11.14
Pte	E.Warner	1st Bedfords	VC – 1.5.15	Killed – 2.5.15
2/Lt	S.C.Woodroffe	8th Rifle Bde	VC – 30.7.15	Killed – 30.7.15
Brig-Gen	C.Fitzclarence	1st Guards Bde	VC – 1899	Killed – 12.11.14

Others whom, over the years, I have come here to remember include:

BROTHERS IN ARMS: There are several pairs of brothers commemorated on the Menin Gate bearing testimony to the tragedy suffered by many families during the Great War; when brothers joined up together, they all too often died together as well. At Ypres, most tragic of all was the triple loss which befell the Rachiel family in May

'Those nameless names' – the interior of the Menin Gate Memorial.

1915. From Holme Road, East Ham, London the three sons had enlisted together as regular soldiers in the 3rd Bn Royal Fusiliers before the war. In August 1914, 3rd Royal Fusiliers were stationed at Lucknow in India and returned to England in December becoming part of 28th Division – one of the last regular army formations to arrive in France, in January 1915. They served initially on the Messines Ridge and during the Second Battle of Ypres were brought up to the fighting north-east of Ypres. The three Rachiel brothers – Arthur, aged twenty-one, Frank aged eighteen and Fred aged twenty-four – were all killed on 24th May 1915 on the Bellewaarde Ridge. A terrible loss under any circumstances, but for none of them to have a grave for the family to visit must have made it even harder to bear.

FUTURE CANADIAN PRIME MINISTER? Talbot Mercier Papineau was a French-Canadian whose grandfather had fought against the British. Well educated, and from the Canadian upper-classes, Papineau practised law before 1914. When war broke out he obtained a commission in Princess Patricia's Canadian Light Infantry (PPCLI); a regiment formed almost entirely from ex-regular British army veterans who had emigrated to Canada. On the voyage out Papineau gave French lessons to his men, and after a brief spell in England his regiment was the first Canadian unit to reach the front line. Papineau was awarded the Military Cross for bravery at St Eloi in March 1915. In 1916 he became a Staff Officer and during the Somme accompanied the Canadian Official Photographer around the battlefield at Courcelette. Frustrated with a desk job, he continually put in requests for a transfer back to the PPCLI but did not re-join his old unit until September 1917 – just prior to the attack on Passchendaele. Promoted Major, he was killed leading his men forward on 30th October 1917, but his body was not retrieved from the battlefield for several weeks. Buried close to the Passchendaele road, the white cross marking his last resting place could not be found when his mother wrote to the IWGC after the war. Despite further explorations, Papineau's body was never found. Prior to the Great War he had been a protégé of the then Canadian Prime Minister, and it is widely considered that, if he had survived, Papineau would

Maj Talbot Papineau MC.

34

himself have eventually taken up this office. Given his French-Canadian background the whole social history of Canada in the twentieth century could have been changed.

GOC MENIN ROAD: Although noted in the list of VCs above, Brigadier General Charles Fitzclarence was a charismatic, brave and well liked senior officer who was far from the 'Lions Led by Donkeys' image of many Great War commanders. Born in 1865, the son of a naval Captain who was also Earl of Munster, he was educated at Eton and Wellington College, and joined the Royal Fusiliers in 1886. Promoted Captain in 1898, Fitzclarence transferred to the Irish Guards and was awarded the VC for three distinct acts of bravery during the Siege of Mafeking in the Boer War. At this time he earned his first nickname, 'The Demon', for his daring in the face of often impossible odds. Rapid promotion followed and he was commanding 1st Irish Guards by 1913, and then a Brigade by the outbreak of war. Just prior to First Ypres he was posted to command 1st Guards Brigade, 1st Division, and was instrumental in organising a brilliant counter-attack near Gheluvelt on 31st October 1914, and as the fighting moved back towards Ypres along the old Roman road he earned another sobriquet, 'GOC Menin Road' – indeed several observers noted that he appeared at times to be running the whole battle. It was this gallant front line leadership which eventually cost him his life on 12th November 1914, whilst advancing at the head of his old regiment near Glencorse Wood.

FROM THE RANKS: 'Gentleman Rankers', well educated men from moneyed families who served in the ranks, were often the stuff of fiction but one is commemorated here – Frederick Charles Jennens Marillier. Born at Fairlight near Hastings, Sussex, in 1888, Marillier was educated at a local minor public school. His father was an artist and his grandfather had been a master at Harrow for fifty years. For a reason that even today remains a mystery, he left the comforts of a well-heeled Edwardian family and joined the Royal Sussex Regiment as a Private in 1912. The life somehow suited him and by 1914 he was a Sergeant. During the fighting on the Aisne in September 1914 he was awarded the Distinguished Conduct Medal for bravery in capturing a German trench during a night attack. Eventually persuaded to take a commission, he was promoted Second Lieutenant in the field. But his service as an officer only lasted a few weeks until his death at Ypres on 30th October 1914.

STRETCHER-BEARER WANTED: The work of the Royal Army Medical Corps is well known, but regimental stretcher-bearers are often forgotten. These were the first port of call for wounded troops in the field. In peacetime these men would make up the battalion band, as the war went on soldiers with enough technical skill and common sense to administer basic medical help replaced them. From the battlefield 'SBs' would carry a wounded soldier back to the Regimental Aid Post to be treated by the battalion Medical Officer. One such stretcher-bearer was Lance Corporal Harry West MM of the 13th Bn Royal Sussex Regiment (3rd South Downs). West was born in Eastbourne, and enlisted with his brother in 1914. He trained as a stretcher-bearer, proceeded overseas in March 1916 and was awarded the Military Medal for bringing in wounded comrades under fire at Richebourg on 30th June – he himself was badly wounded in the process. Returning to his battalion, he served on the Somme, where his brother was killed, and came to Ypres in December 1916. On 31st July 1917, the opening day of Third Ypres, he accompanied the medical officer during the attack on St Julien, and the next day was killed by the same shell which wounded the M.O. An officer in the 13th Royal

Sussex later wrote, 'his untiring efforts for the sick and wounded in the battles in which this battalion has been engaged has simply been beyond praise'.

From the Menin Gate take the road back into the town centre, Meenstraat, which will soon bring you out into the Grote Markt, Cloth Hall and your vehicle.

1 Anon. *The Pilgrims Guide to the Ypres Salient* (For Talbot House c.1920s) p.10.
2 Gordon, H. *The Unreturning Army* (J.M.Dent 1967) p 54
3 6th Bn DCLI *War Diary*, 12.8.15, PRO WO95/1908.
4 A/296th Bde RFA *War Diary*, 25.9.17, PRO WO95/3016.
5 *The Pilgrims Guide to the Ypres Salient* op cit. P.10.
6 Clapham, H.S. *Mud and Khaki* (Hutchinson n.d.) p.130-131.
7 ibid. p.131-132.
8 Gordon op cit. P.54.

Looking towards the ruined centre of Ypres from the Menin Gate in September 1918. TAYLOR LIBRARY

Chapter Two

YSER CANAL WALK – YPRES TO BOESINGHE

STARTING POINT: **Yser canal basin, Ypres**
DURATION: **4¹⁄₂ hours**

WALK SUMMARY: *This walk follows the line of the Yser canal north from Ypres, an area where the front line remained virtually unchanged for over two years. Many small cemeteries are visited en-route along with the dugouts where poet John McCrae wrote 'In Flanders Field' in 1915. Although long, it is a gradual and easy walk, and would suit inexperienced walkers.*

Leave your vehicle close to the Yser canal basin; there is a large tarmac area where vehicles can be parked.

DIXMUDE

10

9   11

8

FRONT LINES 1915-17

German

BRITISH

7

6

1. Yser Canal Basin
2. Duhallow Ads Cem
3. Essex Farm Cem
4. Essex Farm Ads
5. Bard Cottage Cem
6. Hull's Farm
7. Talana Farm Cem
8. Demarcation Stone
9. Robert Bye VC action
10. Artillery Wood Cem
11. Gas Attack Mem

5

4

3

FLYOVER

YSER CANAL

2

N

500m

YPRES

1

A modern view of the Yser canal basin: in the fourteenth century cloth was brought here for sale in the Cloth Hall.

Alternatively, this walk could be started from the Grote Markt in Ypres. In this case, leave the Grote Markt by Diksmuidsestraat. Where this meets the junction of another road, turn left and follow the road right – just round the corner is the Canal basin area.

In the fourteenth century, when Ypres was centre of the European cloth trade, the Yser canal was the means by which cloth was carried to and from Ypres by boat. During the Great War it formed, at various

Fishing in Yser Canal near Boesinghe in January 1918.

points, part of the front line and a multitude of constructions were built into the spoil on the west bank. Makeshift bridges, often destroyed and re-constructed on a daily basis, were placed across the canal where it was behind the British lines. One, made prior to the Passchendaele offensive of July 1917, was strong enough to carry the tanks of the 7th Bn Tank Corps for their attack on St Julien. Today there is no sign of any of these bridges.

From the basin area follow the left edge of the canal basin along Westkaai, past some old factory buildings and warehouses. During the war there were many dumps of equipment and shells around here. At the end of the quay follow a minor tarmac road past an Esso Depot on the left. Soon a wooden footbridge is reached; cross and turn right, following the line of the canal. The canal bank at this point was a major billeting area during the fighting for Ypres. H.S.Clapham described a typical scene when he came to this position with the Honourable Artillery Company in 1915.

> *We...took up our residence in some crazy dugouts on the Yser canal, which we crossed by a pontoon bridge. The dugouts were not even splinter proof, mere shelters from the sun, and along the top of the bank ran a trench, into which we were ordered for shelter whenever shelling started...There is plenty of water in the canal, although it is more or less stagnant. It breeds clouds of mosquitoes, which bite like fun, and though it is nice to be able to get a wash when one likes, there are too many floating carcasses of various sorts.*[1]

As the war went on and it became clear that the front line east of the canal bank was not going to change, these 'crazy dugouts' became more and more permanent in appearance, many being shored up with concrete supports and thick timbers.

Continue along the path and further up, opposite a small concrete quay on the other side of the canal, a small access road appears on the left. Follow this to where it crosses a stream. Stop.

This is the Yserlee, a minor stream that follows the canal. Looking to the left past a new house a grassed embankment is seen. This was the site of Duhallow Advanced Dressing Station (ADS). Constructed in June 1917 by RAMC Field Ambulances of the 39th Division during the period leading up to Third Ypres, it was,

> *...a hive of industry at this time. Dumps of various kinds of shells had been established, whilst battery positions jostled one another the whole way along. It was inevitable that the enemy*

Makeshift bridges across the Yser canal.

should succeed in finding some of these positions. On one such occasion our men were called upon to clear up the gunners. The guns and teams were alike knocked out, one poor youth of eighteen having been blown across the road into a ditch opposite. He was badly wounded and died on the way to the ADS.[2]

During a twenty-four hour period from 31st July 1917 – the opening day of Third Ypres – Duhallow ADS was manned by five medical officers from RAMC units in the 39th Division. The number of casualties treated at this time alone amounted to ninety-four officers and 2,586 other ranks.

Continue along the access road; the nearby military cemetery is soon reached on the right.

DUHALLOW ADS CEMETERY

The cemetery was started just prior to the Third Battle of Ypres in July 1917, as the ADS was established on the canal bank, and was used throughout that offensive, and again until the close of the war. Plots I-IV mark these original graves, some 875 in number, and after the war burials from the surrounding area were brought into the cemetery. Among the 1,560 soldiers buried here are 1,442 British, twenty-six Canadian, thirteen Australian, twelve Newfoundland, six New Zealand, three South African, two British West Indies, two Indian, two French and one Belgian. There are also fifty-four Germans, and Special Memorials to ten British soldiers originally buried in Malakoff Farm Cemetery at Brielen whose graves were destroyed by shellfire. Other Special Memorials exist to twenty-nine men from Fusilier Wood Cemetery at Hollebeke, in the southern sector of the Salient.

The graves reflect the units involved in the opening phase of Third Ypres, in particular those from the 39th Division, and the fighting around Kitchener's Wood and St Julien, are numerous. The Guards and 38th (Welsh) Divisions are also well represented, from their actions at Boesinghe and the Pilckem Ridge. 'A most gallant soldier' – according to the headstone inscription – is buried here. Lieutenant O.Brown (VII-C-20) was a typical cavalry officer; educated at a public school, commissioned from Sandhurst into the 7th Hariana Lancers, Indian Army, he died on the Frezenberg Ridge on 24th April 1915 attached to the 4th Dragoon Guards; his grave was moved to Duhallow after the war. Lieutenant F.M.Drury (III-E-9) of the 1/1st Hertfordshires had first come to Flanders as a private in the Honourable Artillery Company in September 1914, and was wounded three times before being killed on 7th January 1918, still aged only twenty-four.

In Plot II, Row F is a mass grave of forty-one men from the 13th Company Labour Corps who were killed on 9th January 1918 when a truck load of salvaged ammunition from the surrounding area was detonated by a bomb dropped from a German aircraft. Many of the men were attached from other units and the headstones show a variety of cap badges – particularly the Seaforth Highlanders.

From the cemetery return along the access road to the Yser canal towpath. Turn left and continue north. Later on the route passes under a modern road bridge and past this the spoil bank that lined the canal is clearly in evidence. The front line was over to the right about two kilometres distant, beyond the area of the modern factory units. This area of the canal bank was under almost constant shellfire. Further along on the left another access road appears. Here was a main bridge across the Yser, Number 4 Bridge, which also carried a light railway line known on trench maps as La Belle Alliance Tramway. This ran all the way to Buffs Road, north of Wieltje.

Now follow the access road, which becomes cobbled. Just past where the cutting in the spoil bank ends, there is a line of concrete bunkers and sandbags to the right. This is the site of Essex Farm ADS. The cemetery is reached by the same access road, a little further up on the left.

ESSEX FARM CEMETERY & BUNKERS

Probably the most famous and most frequently visited site in the Ypres Salient, Essex Farm was named after a small cottage that stood beside the Boesinghe road at the entrance to the canal access track. When the 4th Division took over this sector in mid-1915 an ADS was established by their RAMC units, and as this division included the 2nd Bn Essex Regiment, the site was probably named by them. The ADS was dug into the canal bank, and at this stage was a primitive timber and elephant iron affair similar to the 'crazy dugouts' near the canal basin as described by Clapham. During Second Ypres it was manned by officers and men from the Canadian Army Medical Corps of 1st (Canadian) Division, who treated many gas cases. One of the officers was Captain John McCrae, an amateur Canadian-born poet who after the death of a friend, and coming out of the ADS one morning to see the ever growing number of wooden crosses, was moved to write the now immortal poem, *In Flanders Fields.*

In Flanders fields the poppies blow
Between the crosses, row on row
That mark our place; and in the sky
The larks, still bravely singing, fly
Scarce heard amid the guns below.

We are the Dead. Short days ago
We lived, felt dawn, saw sunset glow,
Loved and were loved, and now we lie
In Flanders fields.

Take up your quarrel with the foe:
To you from failing hands we throw
The torch; be yours to hold it high.
If ye break faith with us who die
We shall not sleep, though poppies grow
In Flanders fields.

John McCrae submitted the poem to Punch magazine, which subsequently published it, and it soon became world famous. In recognition of this location's importance, the Belgian regional government erected a memorial to McCrae just outside the cemetery and its design has led many people to believe the poet is buried here. However, John McCrae was later promoted and by 1918 was a Lieutenant Colonel at a Base Hospital near Boulogne. Having worn himself out, he died of pneumonia in January that year and was buried in Wimereux Cemetery.

The concrete bunker visible today was built on the site of the original ADS used by McCrae in 1915. Dating from 1916, the ADS was made permanent for the forthcoming Third Ypres offensive – although the nearby Duhallow became the main ADS for this sector at that time. Each chamber in the bunker had their own use (see plan), and the thick concrete must have afforded a great deal of protection from shellfire. Wounded were brought here via communication trenches on the opposite bank of the canal to Number 4 Bridge, and

Essex Farm ADS in 1918.

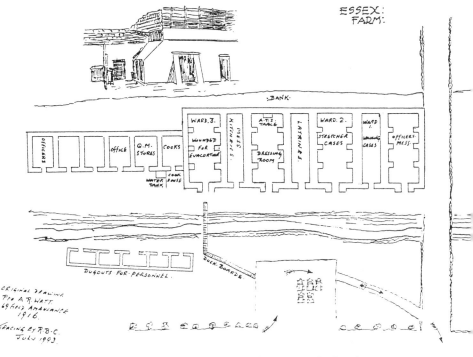

PLAN 1 A wartime plan of Essex Farm showing how each chamber was used. (RAMC Historical Society)

The flooded bunkers before restoration, showing the entrances of each chamber. It was here that the wounded received further treatment after being brought out of the front line. Those who died from their injuries were buried in the adjacent cemetery.

often on the light railway. Once assessed, more serious cases could be evacuated further back via motor ambulances which waited on the Boesinghe road by the ruins of Essex Farm cottage. Graffiti, dating largely from veterans returning to the area after the war, can be found in the last few chambers, as well as a facsimile of the original *In Flanders Fields* poem. Flooded and inaccessible for many years, the bunkers were purchased and restored by the town of Ypres in the early 1990s.

Harry Kendall was serving as a Trooper in 1st King Edward's Horse during Third Ypres and left a graphic description of this area at that time.

> *I...*[was] *stationed for some time on these crossroads near the Essex Farm graveyard. Fritz had a bad habit of sending shells over and ploughing up the graves. For many weeks there was little peace at that end of Essex Farm road – even for the 'glorious' dead. Often a dozen times a day we were smothered over with mud from the graves torn up by Fritz's exhuming shells...Possibly the worst phase of this post by number four bridge was the eternal review of dead men before one's tiring eyes. Slaughtered men lying about in all shapes and forms around this unholy post of ours. Sometimes these immolated human beings...would be wrapped in Army blankets, tied around the head and feet. At other times, nothing but War's frightful disfigurements or mutilations were to be seen on the faces of the bodies of these 'glorious' corpses.*[3]

The Essex Farm Cemetery has 1,088 British, nine Canadian, five German and nineteen unnamed graves. Of these eighty three are unknown and there are nineteen Special Memorials. Plot I is very much a 'comrades cemetery' with distinctive unit plots, in particular from battalions of the 49th (West Riding) Division, whose memorial obelisk is to the rear of the cemetery. This territorial formation from the West Riding of Yorkshire had the distinction of serving along the canal bank sector for the longest continual period. The graves of their men who died here during that time are scattered among the cemeteries south of Boesinghe, many of which will be visited on this walk. Among their casualties in Plot I is a soldier from the West Riding Field Ambulance RAMC who has an interesting inscription on his headstone. The parents of Corporal D.Normington (I-M-17), who died on 12th November 1915, aged twenty-two, chose 'For the love of his wounded comrade he bravely gave his life'.

Essex Farm Cemetery as it appeared shortly after the war.

In another regimental plot, belonging to the Rifle Brigade, the often visited grave of Private Valentine Joe Strudwick (I-U-8) can be found. From Dorking, Surrey, and part of a large family, Strudwick was born on Valentine's Day 1900 and died a month short of his sixteenth birthday when his battalion was shelled in the front line. His body and those of his comrades were brought back to Essex Farm for burial. He is by no means the youngest soldier to die at Ypres – that dubious distinction belongs to Private J. Condon of the 2nd Royal Irish Regiment who is buried in Poelcapelle British Cemetery. His headstone records him as fourteen years old, but an entry in the visitor's book some years ago from an individual who had undertaken research into Condon's life indicated that he was in fact thirteen years and ten months when he died. Nearby is the grave of Private Thomas Barrett VC (I-Z-8) of the 7th Bn South Staffordshire Regiment who died on 27th July 1917. A veteran of Gallipoli and the Somme, Barrett was awarded his VC posthumously for patrol work in No Man's Land against German snipers.

Return to the canal via the access road and continue north along the towpath. This is followed to just before where the canal bends. Another access road is on the left which leads you out onto the main Ypres – Boesinghe road. During the war another trench railway crossed Number 6 Bridge at this point and was known as Lancashire Farm Tramway. It ran from Spahi Farm just behind the British front line. Carefully cross this busy road and turn right, along a footpath to the nearby military cemetery.

BARD COTTAGE CEMETERY

Bard Cottage was a small dwelling between the Ypres road and Yser canal, and close to a bridge bearing the same name. The cemetery was made beyond the spoil bank which gave it protection from German observation in the line some distance away. The first burials were made in June 1915, and the cemetery remained in use until the fighting had moved out of the Salient by October 1918. In particular the graves here reflect the trench service of 38th (Welsh) and 49th (West Riding) Divisions who held the canal bank sector between 1915-17. By Third Ypres there was a large concentration of artillery batteries in the area, and graves from these units are also particularly noticeable. After the war forty-six isolated burials were brought into the cemetery and buried in what is now Plot VI, Row C. Of these some thirty-two were from Marengo Farm Cemetery, which was situated just opposite the access road you used to reach the main road. The majority of the soldiers laid to rest at Marengo Farm were men of the 2nd Bn Seaforth Highlanders and 1st Bn East Lancashire Regiment, killed in June 1915. Like many farms in the area, it acquired its name during the period French troops were on the Yser canal in 1914/15. Today Bard Cottage Cemetery contains the graves of 1,616 British, nine Canadian, six Newfoundland, three British West Indian and two South African soldiers. In addition there are also the graves of three German prisoners who died of wounds, and three Special Memorials.

Rejoin the footpath which borders the road, and go north towards Boesinghe. Further on, as the road bends, stop. Here is a good view to the right towards the tree-lined canal bank. In the fields here was Colenso Farm, and beyond the trees the British front line was only 500 yards away. To the Germans this was dead ground out of view, except from the air, and many field artillery units had their gun positions here. On the left is Hull's Farm, possibly named after Major-General Sir C.P.A.Hull who started the war in the 4th Bn Middlesex Regiment and was a Brigade Staff Officer here during Second Ypres. Born in 1865, he was a long serving regular army officer who went on to command the 56th (London) Division by the time of the Somme in 1916. He survived the war, but died in 1920.

Bard Cottage Cemetery.

Continue along the footpath; a green CWGC sign is seen on the opposite side of the road pointing to a grass path on your left, which leads across the fields to the cemetery.

TALANA FARM CEMETERY

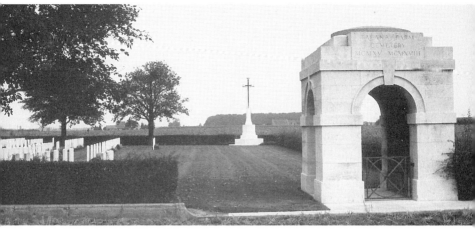

Talana Farm Cemetery.

Two divisions are well represented here. The 4th held this sector after Second Ypres in May 1915 until the summer of that year, and in particular there are many soldiers of the 1st Rifle Brigade. Among them is a Warrant Officer who had been awarded a Military Cross for bravery: CSM W.Halliwell MC (I-E-8), who was killed on 6th July 1915. The other division was the 49th (West Riding) which took over this sector in August 1915, after the 4th had gone south to the Somme. Burials from Third Ypres in 1917 include a row of four officers all killed on the same day. These made up the headquarters of 9th Bn Northumberland Fusiliers; their dugout at Stray Farm on the Pilckem Ridge was struck by a single shell, killing the commanding officer, adjutant, medical officer and intelligence officer. They are buried left to right, with Lieutenant Colonel A.Bryant DSO (III-K-1) being the

The graves of the headquarters of 9th Bn Northumberland Fusiliers who were killed on 17th October 1917.

first grave. He was a regular in the Gloucestershire Regiment, attached to the battalion[4].

Returning to the footpath continue to Boesinghe. The village itself is reached by forking left further on, opposite a white modern bungalow on the right. This road leads you directly into the centre of Boesinghe.

The Boesinghe sector was taken over from the French in mid-1915 by units of the 4th Division; thereafter it remained the left flank of the British army on the Western Front. The small village of the same name was just west of the Yser canal, and boasted a large ornate chateau which was used thereafter as brigade headquarters for units in the line here. Field Ambulances also set up an ADS in the chateau grounds, and several military cemeteries were established around the village, one in the chateau park itself. The large BLOCKHOUSE was used as an observation post, and as all the surrounding houses at that time were knocked flat by shellfire it afforded good views towards the German trenches across the canal. Today it is surmounted by a German Minnenwerfer trench mortar, which fired the larger version of the much feared 'Minnies' known to all British soldiers. In front is a DEMARCATION STONE, one of several in the Ypres Salient marking the limit of the German advance in April 1918. This one bears a

Boesinghe village c.1915.

TRENCH MORTAR

Veurne 28
Poperinge 12
Elverdinge 8

The concrete bunker, now covered in Ivy, and the Demarcation Stone at Boesinghe.

Belgian helmet, as it was men from the Belgian army who defended the village at that time. Although the Germans crossed the Yser canal, Boesinghe itself did not fall but became part of the front line until September 1918.

Take the road directly opposite the bunker, Brugstraat, and follow it to the main road. At the end cross via an indicated crossing opposite an old mill. This will lead you via a footpath onto the Boesinghe canal bridge.

The front line ran through this area from 1915 until just prior to the Third Ypres offensive. Looking north, for some time the allied trenches were on the left bank and the Germans on the right. British divisions which served in this sector suffered many casualties from the day to day activities of trench warfare, more so as the lines were so close at this point. In the weeks leading up to the 31st July 1917 attack a plan was made to move the front line eastwards across the canal, and thus make it a more favourable position to

A front line trench in the Yser canal sector, 1917.

51

advance from. Units from the Guards Division were selected for this operation, and in the days leading up to it the German front line was saturated with gas shells fired from 4,000 Livens projectors of the Special Companies Royal Engineers. In the final phase this bombardment was increased when 4.5-inch Howitzers fired further gas shells onto strong points and woods, along the banks of the Steenbeek river to the rear of the German lines. The 49th (Reserve) Division holding the German outposts were driven to breaking point by the gas and by 24th July 1917 realised their position was no longer tenable and withdrew to trenches nearer Artillery Wood. British patrols confirmed this the day after and the line moved forward, across the canal, with few casualties. By 27th July over 3,000 yards length and 500 yards depth of former German positions were now in British hands; enabling the Guards Division to launch their attack on 31st July without having to cross the canal first and thereby no doubt saving many lives.

Continue across the canal bridge, and as the road bends right, take a minor road directly opposite. Follow it. The ground to the right of this

A modern aerial view of Boesinghe and the Yser canal.

road was where the 1st Welsh Guards advanced on 31st July 1917. Sergeant R.Bye was awarded a Victoria Cross for his bravery here on that day; when pushing forward he captured several strong points during the attack on Artillery Wood and killed, wounded or captured over seventy Germans. Bye's VC was gazetted some weeks later, and he survived the war.

At the end of the minor road turn right into Poelstraat, which leads you to the military cemetery, further up on the right.

ARTILLERY WOOD CEMETERY

Artillery Wood Cemetery in the 1920s.

On a site just north of Artillery Wood (which was never replanted), this ground was attacked and captured by the 2nd Guards Brigade on 31st July 1917. The Guards established a small 'comrades' graveyard here at that time, and it was then used by other units as a front line cemetery for the operations across Pilckem Ridge. Burials continued until March 1918, and by the conclusion of the war there were 141 graves of which forty-two are men from artillery units who had their gun sites nearby as the fighting moved forward. In the 1920s the cemetery was enlarged by the inclusion of 1,154 burials from the Boesinghe – Pilckem Ridge battlefield; many of them came from the cemetery located in the grounds of Boesinghe Chateau. Today the graves number: 1,243 British, thirty Canadian, ten Newfoundland, five Australian, two New Zealand and one South African. There are twelve Special Memorials and of the total number 506 are unknown.

Every regiment of Foot Guards is represented in this cemetery, giving it very much a Guards Division feel. Among them are comrades

'Hedd Wyn' : the grave of Pte E.H. Evans at Artillery Wood.

from Robert Bye's 1st Welsh Guards. The second most represented unit is the 38th (Welsh) Division which attacked on the right flank of the Guards on 31st July. The most famous of these burials is Private Elas Evans (II-F-11) of 15th Bn Royal Welsh Fusiliers who died of wounds in a regimental aid post on the Pilckem Ridge that day, aged thirty. Better known as 'Hedd Wyn', Evans was arguably the most famous and important twentieth century poet who wrote in Welsh, and his grave continues to attract many visitors.

Nearby is another Great War poet, Francis Ledwidge (II-B-5), who was one of Irelands' most important twentieth century poets. Ledwidge was born at Slane, County Meath, in August 1887 into a large Irish family. His father died when he was five and they lived in poverty for many years. Leaving school at fourteen he worked first as a farm labourer and then on the roads. In his spare time he wrote poetry; his first published poem appeared in 1910, leading to a collection in book form. Ledwidge joined the 5th Bn Royal Inniskilling Fusiliers in October 1914 and served at Gallipoli the following year. After being evacuated back to England with sickness in 1916, he transferred to the 1st Bn and fought at Arras and then at Ypres. Like Evans, he also died on 31st July 1917, when his battalion was on working parties near Boesinghe. In the pouring rain Francis Ledwidge had stopped to have a welcome cup of tea. Almost immediately a stray shell exploded close by, killing him instantly.

Leaving the cemetery turn right at the end of Pozelstraat, stopping on the right-hand corner.

This is one of several gas attack memorials in the Salient, in this case commemorating men of the 45th (Algerian) and 87th (Territorial) Divisions of the French army who were on the left flank of the British lines when gas was used for the first time on 22nd April 1915. Overwhelmed by the poisonous cloud, the French troops understandably ran – and suffered many casualties. The ancient Breton Calvary, which forms the centre point of the memorial, indicates the territorial regiments were from Brittany; the surrounding stones were specially brought up from the region after the war. There is also a very

The lockgates on the Yser canal; by 1915 the front lines were either side of the canal at this point.

good bronze orientation table, but the planting of trees on the site has somewhat obscured the view.

Leaving the memorial turn right in the direction of Boesinghe and continue along the main road until another road is seen on the left, sign-posted for Ypres (Ieper). Turn off here following the footpath. It soon crosses the road and takes you down another footpath to the old railway bridge. Cross this and turn left. The lock and lock-house are reached and from here follow the towpath back along the canal to Ypres. It is about four kilometres, taking just over an hour at average speed, and retracing your steps to the canal basin and your vehicle, or further into Ypres itself. An alternative route if the walker does not wish to walk back to Ypres would be to return to Brugestraat in Boesinghe, where a bus stop and shelter are found. Here fairly frequent buses run to Ypres.

1 Clapham, H.S. *Mud and Khaki* (Hutchinson n.d.) p.186.
2 Jobson, A. *Via Ypres* (Westminster Publishing Co Ltd 1934) p.98.
3 Kendall, H. *A New York Actor On The Western Front* (Christopher Publishing House 1932) p.73-74.
4 See 9th Bn Northumberland Fusiliers *War Diary,* 17.10.17, PRO WO95/2466.

Communication trench, Sanctuary Wood. H.A.C. sector, June 1915.

Chapter Three

SANCTUARY WOOD – HOOGE – BELLEWAARDE RIDGE WALK

STARTING POINT: **Trench museum, Hill 62, Sanctuary Wood.**
DURATION: **3¹/₂ hours (excluding time spent in museums).**

WALK SUMMARY: *This route follows some of the most important ground around the Menin Road on the centre 'bulge' of the Salient. Heavy fighting took place here in 1915, and the front lines barely changed for another two years. The area of mining activity on the Bellewaarde Ridge is also visited.*

Park your vehicle in the car park of Sanctuary Wood trench museum. It is suggested that you visit the museum first, as it has many photographs and maps relating to the area covered by this walk.

SANCTUARY WOOD TRENCH MUSEUM was started by the grandfather of the present owner, the well-known Jacques Scheer. Sanctuary Wood was the name given to a wood south of the Menin Road where, during First Ypres, men isolated from their units gathered together before going back up the line. The area was also used to screen units going up to the front, as it did not directly come into the

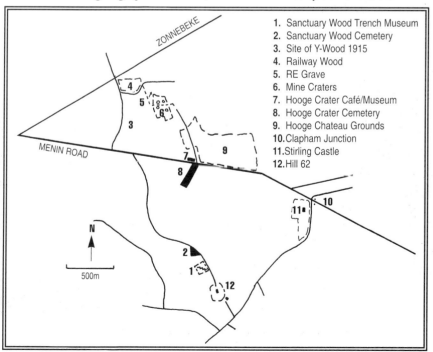

1. Sanctuary Wood Trench Museum
2. Sanctuary Wood Cemetery
3. Site of Y-Wood 1915
4. Railway Wood
5. RE Grave
6. Mine Craters
7. Hooge Crater Café/Museum
8. Hooge Crater Cemetery
9. Hooge Chateau Grounds
10. Clapham Junction
11. Stirling Castle
12. Hill 62

battle area until the end of First Ypres, being shelled for the first time on the night of 13th/14th November 1914. By 1915 it was part of the front line on the nearest low ridge to Ypres. This high ground from Hill 62 to Hooge and the Bellewaarde Ridge commanded the positions before the town and from 1915, until it was finally taken from the Germans in the opening phase of Third Ypres, there was a great deal of fighting for the possession and re-possession of this area. An officer of the 13th Bn Canadian Infantry (Royal Highlanders of Canada) described the scene here in June 1916.

> *Sanctuary Wood was by this time a wood in name only. Such trees as stood were riven and leafless, while their fallen branches added to the maze of wire and trenches beneath. The air was heavy with the sickening odour of decay, so that the whole battered district, even by day, was a place of grisly horror and evil omen.*[1]

Inside the main museum building is a wide array of battlefield relics, weapons equipment and uniforms. Photographs of the area are also on display, but perhaps the most popular feature, if popular is the right word, is the stereoscopic viewers dating from the 1920s. These show three-dimensional black and white images, largely from French and German sources, which are among the most harrowing you are ever likely to see. Some are truly gruesome, and those of a nervous disposition might find them too disturbing to look at. They present a side of the war rarely seen in British collections.

Outside, in the wood itself, are the remains of a British second line trench system dating from around 1915/16. Comparing contemporary

Sappers of the 1/1st Cheshire Field Coy RE dig-in under fire in Sanctuary Wood, 1915.

trench maps the trenches here seem to be part of the Lover's Walk, Artillery Place and Warrington Avenue sector. Major R.T.Rees, 8th Bn Loyal North Lancs, called Lover's Walk a 'filthy ditch' in late 1915, and today it often still lives up to this reputation! Visitors take a signposted route round the wood following a zigzagged main second line trench (Lover's Walk). Here and there are fire-bays, trench mortar positions, remains of dugouts and funk holes, and about half way along is the entrance to a tunnel. Concrete lining has replaced the wartime wooden shoring, and although often wet and muddy, the tunnel is safe to walk through and lit all the way along. Inside it branches: to the right it joins a communication trench (Artillery Place), to the left it once continued all the way to the front line on Hill 62; but now it comes out near some shell holes on the edge of the wood. Duckboards, sandbags and of course the smell and noise of war are missing, but visitors often find this among the most evocative places anywhere in the Ypres Salient today. Back in the museum relics, postcards and souvenirs are on sale, as well as books – among them the *Battleground Europe* series[2].

Leaving the museum turn left and follow the road – known as Maple Avenue – to a military cemetery further along on the left.

SANCTUARY WOOD BRITISH CEMETERY

There were three military cemeteries in Sanctuary Wood by 1916, containing fifty-six, fifty-five and one hundred graves respectively from the May – August 1915 period. All of them were virtually obliterated in the fighting for Hill 62 in June 1916 when this ground was swept by shellfire. Traces of the second cemetery remained after the war when battlefield clearance parties returned, and this became the nucleus of the present cemetery (now Plot I). This original cemetery had been expanded by 1918 to 137 graves, including forty-one Canadians and one German. Due to wartime damage, the exact location of many of these burials could not be ascertained and today eighty-eight of them are commemorated by Special Memorials at the rear of the cemetery Plots II – V were added between 1927 and 1932, when 1,852 war graves were brought in from a wide area around the Ypres Salient – in some cases from as far away as Nieuport on the Belgian coast. The total number of commemorations are therefore: 1,734 British, 142 Canadian, eighty-eight Australian, eighteen New Zealand, three South African, three Newfoundland, and one German. Of these 1,353 are unidentified – nearly eighty percent.

The most frequently visited grave in Sanctuary Wood British

Lieutenant Gilbert Talbot.

Cemetery is that of Lieutenant Gilbert Talbot (I-G-1) who was killed at Hooge with 7th Rifle Brigade on 30th July 1915. The son of the Lord Bishop of Winchester, Gilbert Talbot's brother, Neville, was a great friend of fellow army chaplain, Rev. P.B. 'Tubby' Clayton who had been serving in the Salient with 6th Division. In an old town house at Poperinghe, the two men established in late 1915 an 'oasis' behind the front line for soldiers out on rest, which they christened 'Talbot House' after Gilbert Talbot. It is still there today – see Poperinghe Town Walk.

Plot I originally contained many graves of units from 14th (Light) Division who fought in the Hooge – Sanctuary Wood sector in mid-1915. Among them are five officers from the 6th Bn Duke of Cornwall's Light Infantry (DCLI) who were killed at Zouave Wood on 30th/31st July 1915 (see below): Captain F.M.Aston (I-C-4), Lieutenant W.E.H.Birch (Sp Mem), Second Lieutenant A.C.Challoner (I-C-9), Lieutenant F.E.B.Hulton-Sams (Sp Mem) and Lieutenant G.M.Paddison (Sp Mem).

Outside the cemetery is a private memorial to Lieutenant Thomas Keith Hedley Rae, who died at the Hooge craters on 30th July 1915 with 8th Rifle Brigade – a sister battalion of Gilbert Talbot's 7th Bn, and also serving in the 14th (Light) Division. Rae's body was never found and his name is commemorated on the Menin Gate, but after the war his family paid for this cross to be erected in the grounds of Hooge chateau, close to the spot where he was last seen. In the 1970s the last direct descendant of the family who owned Hooge chateau asked for the memorial to be moved to a place where it could be properly tended, and it was then the CWGC took over responsibility and relocated it here.

Return to Maple Avenue and turn left continuing in the direction of the Menin Road. Further along, as the road bends, there are good views to your right, towards Hooge and Hooge Crater Cemetery – visited later in the walk. Stop here.

Zouave Wood once stood in these fields; roughly between the road you are on and Hooge Crater Cemetery. There was heavy fighting here in July 1915 when the 14th (Light) Division – a formation originally raised during the Peninsular War – fought for the possession of Bellewaarde Ridge, Hooge, and Zouave and Sanctuary Woods. The Germans used flame-throwers in this action for the first time on the Western Front, when on 30th July 1915 a number of units in the division came up against several of them. One of those involved was

6th Bn DCLI who advanced on Zouave Wood and despite heavy casualties managed to take the position. Above them, as the ground sloped up to Hooge, were the Germans – but 6th DCLI were ordered to hold on at all costs. For the next two days they were subjected to bombing attacks, infantry assaults and continuous shellfire. It was only when flame-throwers were used that men from C Company fell back. Sergeant Silver of the battalion machine-gun section called out; 'If you don't get back to your line, I'll open fire on you. The 6th Cornwalls are damned well going to stick it '[3] At midnight on 31st July what was left of 6th DCLI handed over the position intact.

Continue along Maple Avenue until it meets the Menin Road.

The Menin Road from Ypres up to Hooge was a busy thoroughfare throughout the war years, and was heavily tunnelled in 1915 by Engineers from the 14th (Light) Division who were in the Hooge sector at that time. In 1930, when the road was undergoing repairs, and after particularly heavy rain, a whole section collapsed just east of Hell Fire Corner and another close to Birr Cross Roads. On the site of a former underground dressing station, the resulting hole was fifty feet across and forty feet deep.

Carefully cross the busy road at this point, and go towards Ypres on the pavement on the other side. A little further along a minor road appears on the right, Begijnenbos Straat, with a green CWGC sign for RE Grave. Turn right here and follow the road uphill to just before some farm buildings on the left. Stop here.

Y Wood was located in the fields to the right of this road, and the ground rises up to some woods which are on the crest of Bellewaarde

A contemporary illustration of the fighting at Hooge on 16th June 1915.

Ridge. The Cross of Sacrifice of RE Grave can also be seen. Y Wood was a position captured by the Germans in early 1915 and assaulted by the 1st Honourable Artillery Company and other units of 3rd Division on 16th June 1915. H.S.Clapham described the fighting that day as '... full of horrors and I feel almost competent to write another story of the descent into Hell.'[4] His battalion had got into the German front line and consolidated its position. Flags were used to indicate progress in the attack and some were seen in the second line. It was then that a whistle blew and Clapham's company was moved out into No Man's Land. He found the forward trenches full of dead, and the order came round to dig in. Clapham and his comrades began the laborious task of moving the barbed wire from the old German parapet onto the parados. Sandbags were filled and new communication trenches dug – but the captured lines were pummelled by German artillery and casualties mounted. A German attack followed a further heavy bombardment, but it was beaten back. Eventually relieved, Clapham noted,

> '...we have lost half the battalion and nearly all our officers, including the Colonel and Second-in-Command. Those of us who are left look worn and old, and our nerves are in tatters.'[5]

Continue on the road uphill until it meets another minor road on the right. Turn right and stop by the wood on your left.

This is Railway Wood. So named since it bordered on the Ypres – Roulers railway line (now a fast road link to Zonnebeke), Railway Wood was part of the front line by 1915 and fought over several times; mining activity was prominent in this part of the Salient. For many

A modern aerial view of the Bellewaarde Ridge where the front lines were in 1915. (John Giles)

years there were several small mine craters in the Railway Wood area, now only a handful remain as farmers filled them in. Major William 'Billy' Congreve, the son of a Victoria Cross winner who would himself win a posthumous VC on the Somme in 1916, visited the sector just after the 16th June 1915 attack.

> *Eventually we worked our way round to Railway Wood. Here the mess was very bad. Also the Germans were very close, only about fifteen yards. A burial party of some sixty men arrived and got to work... Everything was quiet while we were up there, hardly any snipers at work in the German lines and no shelling. There is no doubt about the value of the ground gained. Looking back towards Ypres from the trench between Railway Wood and Y Wood, one can see every bit of ground.*[6]

From the same position today the view afforded to Billy Congreve is quite apparent – and the importance of these low ridges around Ypres and why both sides fought for their possession clearly realised.

Continue down the minor road which runs alongside Railway Wood. Although there are signs of shell holes inside, it is private property and cannot be entered. Part of the wood now has a house built in it. As the road bends, there is a cart track on the right, with a CWGC signpost for RE Grave. Follow this to the Cross of Sacrifice visible in the fields.

RE GRAVE, RAILWAY WOOD

Located on ground that was the apex of the fighting here, RE Grave (Royal Engineers Grave) is a unique military cemetery. There are no headstones here – just a Cross of Sacrifice on the base of which are recorded the names of twelve men. All died below ground in tunnelling operations on the Bellewaarde Ridge and at Hooge between 14th December 1915 and 22nd July 1917; their bodies lost or buried in the maze of tunnels and galleries below where you are now. Some of these men were Royal Engineers, others transferred or on loan from infantry units - a common practice. The main inscription reads,

RE Grave in the 1920s.

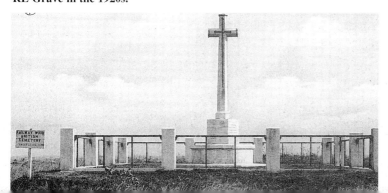

Beneath this spot lie the bodies of an officer, three NCOs and eight men of, or attached to, the 177th Tunnelling Company RE who were killed in action underground during the defence of Ypres.

Around RE Grave is evidence of these mining operations; small craters, often filled with water are only a short distance away but are usually wired off and are on private ground. Under a new Belgian law these are now protected as historical monuments, and cannot be filled in.

Return via the path to the cart track and turn left, following it left again into the woods. Stay on the track through the woods past a farm until it joins a metalled track going south. Follow this to the Menin Road. On the right, just before the main road, is a museum/café.

HOOGE CRATER CAFÉ & MUSEUM

This recent museum is situated on the former No Man's Land at Hooge where several large mine craters obliterated this section of the Menin Road during the war. The scene here was one of utter desolation, a morass of shell holes and craters, and a typical account is that of the 2nd Leinsters in August 1915.

'The Leinsters lay astride the Menin Road round the lips of the crater with both flanks in the air. The inside of this vast crater presented a terrible appearance; the enemy had turned it into a honeycomb of dugouts during the period when they held it. Tier upon tier of dugouts made from lines of railway sleepers – yet this cover did not save them from our guns: it became a veritable death trap. Fully 200 mangled German corpses lay in the crater, and after the Leinsters had completely consolidated the new line they had the task of filling in this crater with lime and earth. Not a blade of grass was visible on this shell-pitted and bleached-up terrain of the Hooge Ridge.'[7]

The museum is located inside an old school and chapel, and entrance is gained via the café. The exhibits are arranged around a series of life size dioramas depicting various aspects of the Ypres Salient. Maps and photographs abound, and near the old entrance is an amazing collection of shells and ordnance from all nations and of all calibres! The weight alone must be staggering and the combined explosive effect of these pieces when live unimaginable. Thankfully they are now deactivated! Outside are field guns and other large pieces. The café owner, Roger, is a friendly character and welcomes English visitors. A range of battlefield relics, postcards and books are on sale, and the café provides refreshments and light lunches and snacks. It also has good, clean toilets. Well worth a visit.

Leaving the museum carefully cross the Menin Road to the military cemetery opposite.

HOOGE CRATER CEMETERY

Another of the larger cemeteries in the Salient, burials were started here during Third Ypres by the 7th Division in October 1917. The area was then still littered with mine craters, and a small plot of seventy-six graves existed by 1918. These are now in Plot I, Rows A to D. After the war it was selected as a site for one of the main concentration cemeteries and 5,800 graves were moved to it. These and the originals now total: 5,153 British, 509 Australian, 119 New Zealand, ninety-five Canadian, and two British West Indies Regiment. Of these 3,580 are unknowns – over half. There are also forty-five Special Memorials.

This is one of the largest concentrations of Australian Imperial Force (AIF) graves in the Salient, and an AIF Victoria Cross winner is buried here. Private Patrick Joseph Bugden (VII-C-5), from New South Wales, was serving with the 31st Bn AIF and was awarded a posthumous VC for bravery in Polygon Wood in September 1917. His citation reads,

> *For conspicuous bravery and devotion to duty when, on two occasions, our advance was temporarily held up by strongly held pillboxes. Private Budgen, in the face of devastating fire from machine-guns, gallantly led small parties to attack these strong points, and, successfully silencing the machine-guns with bombs, captured the garrison at the point of the bayonet. On another occasion, when a Corporal, who had become detached from his company, had been captured and was taken to the rear by the enemy, Private Bugden single-handed, rushed to the rescue of his comrade, shot one enemy and bayoneted the remaining two,*

Hooge Crater Cemetery in the 1920s.

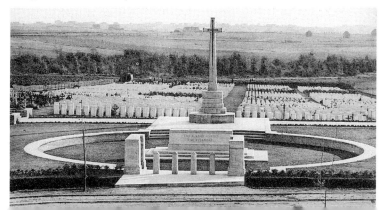

thus releasing the Corporal. On five occasions he rescued wounded men under intense shell and machine-gun fire, showing an utter contempt and disregard for danger. Always foremost in volunteering for any dangerous mission, it was in the execution of one of these missions that this gallant soldier was killed.'

Leaving the cemetery, carefully re-cross the road, and turn right, going east along the Menin Road, following the path. A few hundred yards further on, still on the left, and set back from the road, is Hooge chateau. It is now a hotel-restaurant and can be visited by following the main entrance into the grounds.

Hooge chateau was one of the largest such buildings in the Salient, with extensive grounds that backed onto the Bellewaarde Ridge. Destroyed by 1918, the current building is roughly on the site of the original chateau stables. During First Ypres Hooge chateau was used as a headquarters by 1st and 2nd Divisions. Disaster struck at the height of the battle on 31st October 1914 when two shells pitched through the roof dramatically interrupting a staff meeting. Major General S.H.Lomax, commanding 1st Division, was so badly wounded by the blast he never really recovered and died some months later in England. Six senior staff officers were killed instantly, another dying of his wounds, and two others wounded. NCOs and men attached to the staff and assisting in the conference were also injured. At such a crucial point in the battle it seemed that the situation might be lost with the death and wounding of so many important officers, but Major General Monro, commanding 2nd Division, despite being blown off his feet, went back to command his men and the Germans were held on the

German trenches at Hooge Crater c.1915.

Phot. H. Ierchel

Menin Road. Those killed in this incident were taken back to Ypres Town Cemetery and buried together[8].

Hooge chateau eventually fell to the Germans, but by 1915 it had become part of the front line and mining operations began. Evidence of these craters can still be seen in the chateau grounds today. The lines moved to-and-fro in June, July and August 1915, and on 25th September another large-scale attack was launched by the 3rd Division as a diversionary attack for the Battle of Loos, then being fought in northern France. H.S.Clapham described the scene in his diary just prior to the operation.

The ground all round was in a horrible condition, churned and flung up in small hillocks, overlooking evil-smelling water-holes. It was strewn with bones, broken tools, burst sandbags, and pieces of torn clothing.[9]

The 2nd Bn Middlesex Regiment were also participating in this attack, and one of their officers, Lieutenant R.P.Hallowes, was awarded a posthumous Victoria Cross for his bravery. Hallowes was born in Redhill, Surrey, and educated at Haileybury College. He was an early member of the then fledgling Boy Scouts movement, shot at Bisley for his college, and joined the Artists' Rifles (a territorial battalion of the London Regiment) in 1909, while working as assistant manager of the Mansel Tin-Plate Works. He proceeded overseas with the Artists' Rifles in December 1914, and was commissioned when the unit became an OTC, being gazetted in April 1915 to the Middlesex Regiment. The area around Hooge was well known to him; Hallowes was awarded the Military Cross for his bravery in the fighting here on 19th July 1915. His citation for the operations of 25th September onwards reads,

For most conspicuous bravery and devotion to duty during the fighting at Hooge...Second Lieutenant Hallowes displayed throughout these days the greatest bravery and untiring energy, and set a magnificent example to his men during four heavy and prolonged bombardments. On more than one occasion he climbed up on to the parapet, utterly regardless of danger, in order to put fresh heart into his men. He made daring reconnaissance of German positions in our lines. When a supply of bombs was running short he went back under very heavy shellfire and brought up a fresh supply. Even after he was mortally wounded he continued to cheer those around him and to inspire them with fresh courage.[10]

Rupert Hallowes leading his men over the top at Hooge on 25th September 1915.

The words of encouragement he shouted to his men echoed those of the Colonel of the 57th Foot (later Middlesex Regiment) over a hundred years before at Albuera during the Peninsula War, when he urged his men to 'Die Hard'; thus earning the regiment the name 'The Die-Hards'. That same call was repeated by Hallowes here at Hooge. Badly wounded, Rupert Hallowes was evacuated back to Ypres where he died of wounds on 30th September 1915, aged thirty-four. After the war his grave was moved to Bedford House Cemetery – see The Bluff Walk.

The Hooge chateau grounds are accessible to the public; the chateau itself has a good bar serving refreshments. By the side of the large water-filled crater is a German pillbox dating from 1916, repaired and later used by the British after the ground was captured on 31st July 1917 by units of the 8th Division. But do bear in mind this is a working hotel and guests will be staying here.

Returning to the Menin Road, turn left and continue eastwards, keeping to the footpath/cycle path – beware of cyclists! Soon the Bellewaarde Amusement Park is reached on the left. Just outside, by the road, is a regimental memorial.

This commemorates the officers and men of the King's Royal Rifle Corps who fought and died in the Ypres Salient, 1914-18. Another of the same design exists on the Somme; two great killing grounds of the Western Front which claimed the lives of many riflemen. Now dwarfed by the huge car park attached to the Amusement Park, some pilgrims might find it a touch ironic that such a place exists in the middle of a place where so many men fought and died. Others might see it as a good thing.

Staying on the Menin Road continue eastwards for another kilometre, past some woodland on the right, until a road junction is reached. Memorials can be seen both sides of the main road.

This place was known as Clapham Junction on British maps. In

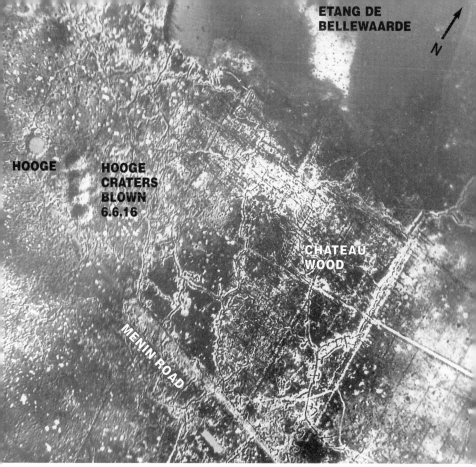

An aerial view of the Hooge chateau grounds and craters, 1916. (Ed Storey)

1914 the 1st Bn Gloucestershire Regiment fought here, and the obelisk left of the road commemorates them. The other memorial is to the 18th (Eastern) Division, considered by many military historians as one of the finest British divisions which served on the Western Front. Other divisional memorials exist on the Somme, where it was one of the only divisions to achieve all its objectives on 1st July 1916. The 18th fought here at Ypres in July and August 1917, when Captain Harold Ackroyd MC RAMC, medical officer to the 6th Bn Royal Berkshires, was awarded a Victoria Cross for bravery in tending the wounded in the opening stage of Third Ypres. He was sniped and killed in Jargon Trench, near Glencorse Wood; his body was brought further back for burial in Birr Cross Roads Cemetery.

Leaving the Menin Road go south on the road by the 18th Division memorial, Pappotstraat. Although it is private, and access

69

All that was left of Hooge chateau in 1919.

cannot be gained, in the woodland on the right of this road was the wartime location of Stirling Castle.

Stirling Castle was the name given to a small chateau set in wooded grounds south of the Menin Road. The area was fought over during First Ypres and then captured by the Germans; the chateau then remaining behind their lines until 1917. By the opening stage of Third Ypres, the ruins of the chateau were reinforced with several concrete bunkers. The position was attacked by 90th Brigade, 30th Division, on 31st July 1917, when men of the Manchester Pals battalions advanced under heavy fire but lost direction. The 17th Bn King's Liverpool Regiment (Liverpool Pals) then came up, but it was units from 21st Brigade which finally cleared Stirling Castle that day, and held a new defence line east of it; with their left flank on the Menin Road at Clapham Junction. Today the chateau is rebuilt and a private residence, but at certain times of the year signs of shell holes and trenches can be seen amongst the trees. Sadly one cannot freely wander through them.

Pappotstraat was known as Green Jacket Ride on British trench maps, as it was near here that the King's Royal Rifle Corps, who in Napoleonic times had worn green jackets as uniforms, fought in 1914. The regiment had two battalions in Flanders at this time; the 1st Bn alone lost 1,037 officers and men by the close of First Ypres[11].

Continue south on Pappotstraat for about two kilometres. Just before a large modern farm ahead to the left, and at a bend in the road, a tarmac track is seen on the right, leading off to a small farmhouse. Follow this to the metal farm gate. At the end, go left and follow a small footpath going off at an angle. This brings you via a gap in the hedge, and past the gardener's hut, into the grounds of Hill 62 Canadian Memorial.

The Canadian memorial on Hill 62 in the 1920s.

The action at Hill 62 in June 1916 was known to the Canadians as The Battle of Mount Sorrel and became one of the Canadian Expeditionary Force's (CEF) battle honours. Hill 62 was one of the few remaining pieces of high ground on the ridge immediately east of Ypres still in British hands, and the Germans were determined to take it. At just after 6am on 2nd June 1916 an attack on the Canadian positions was launched, part of a large attack from Hooge, through Hill 62, Mount Sorrel to Observatory Ridge. Hill 62 was held by 3rd (Canadian) Division, and an intense artillery bombardment of their lines smashed a hole in the defences through which over 8,000 German soldiers – largely Wurtemberger units – poured in and took the high ground. During the fighting Major General Mercer, commanding 3rd Division, was killed and a brigade commander wounded. Casualties were heavy; the 4th Canadian Mounted Rifles alone lost 640 men. A counter-attack was organised the same day using battalions from both 2nd and 3rd (Canadian) Divisions, but it was thrown back with heavy losses. Fighting continued, and on 6th June further positions were taken by the Germans. Sir Julian Byng, commanding the Canadian Corps, organised a well-planned counter-stroke, which was executed on 13th June. Despite poor weather, the CEF managed to push the Germans back to their original start line.

The site on Hill 62 was one of a number selected after the war as a site to commemorate the principal Canadian actions on the Western Front. With the exception of Vancouver Corner, near St Julien, all are of the same design and each stone bears an inscription in English and the local language indicating which action is commemorated. Hill 62 is one of the largest Canadian sites in the Salient, and Maple Avenue, along which you have already walked, was specially constructed after the war to link it with the Menin Road.

From the memorial walk back down to the car park of Sanctuary Wood Trench Museum, and your vehicle.

1 Featherstonhaugh, R.C. *The 13th Battalion Royal Highlanders of Canada 1914-1919* (By the Regiment 1925) p.109.
2 Among them is Nigel Cave's *Sanctuary Wood & Hooge* (Pen & Sword 1993) which covers the area of this walk in some detail.
3 Brice, B. *The Battle Book of Ypres* (John Murray 1927) p.260.
4 Clapham, H.S. *Mud and Khaki* (Hutchinson n.d.) p.141.
5 ibid. p.157.
6 Norman, T. *Armageddon Road: A VC's Diary 1914-16* (William Kimber 1982) p.152.
7 Brice op cit. p.158.
8 Brice op cit. p.141 and *War Diary* 2nd Division Headquarters, 31.10.14, PRO WO95/1283.
9 Clapham op cit. p.210.
10 *London Gazette*, 16th November 1915.
11 Figures given in Anon. *The King's Royal Rifle Corps Chronicle 1914* (Warren & Son 1915) p.138.

Chapter Four

ZILLEBEKE WALK

STARTING POINT: **Transport Farm (Railway Dugouts) Cemetery.**
DURATION: **3¹/₂ hours.**

WALK SUMMARY: *A fairly short walk across easy ground, this route is suitable for novice or first time walkers. It covers the area around the important village of Zillebeke, close to and part of the front line almost continuously between 1914 and 1918.*

Park your vehicle outside Transport Farm Cemetery. It is easily reached from Ypres either on foot or by car via the Lille Gate, and turning off at Shrapnel Corner on the Armentieres road.

TRANSPORT FARM (RAILWAY DUGOUTS) CEMETERY:

Transport Farm was the name given to a collection of buildings close to the Ypres – Comines railway line. Its name probably originates from the fact that battalions in the line around Zillebeke or Hill 60 had their transport lines in the vicinity. At this point the railway line is on a high embankment and British soldiers soon dug into the sides creating dugouts and stores, and an Advanced Dressing Station was established by 1916; these were marked on British maps as Railway Dugouts ADS. Burials began during Second Ypres in April 1915, and increased once the ADS opened; many graves were damaged by shellfire during 1917, and again in 1918 when the front line was close by. By the end of the war there were 1,705 burials; 258 of them were destroyed and no longer marked. When the cemetery was made permanent these were commemorated with Special Memorials. A further 423 graves were brought in from the surrounding area in the 1920s making the total commemorations: 1,629 British, 594 Canadian, 154 Australian, four Indian, four German prisoners, three New Zealanders, two whose units was unknown, and one British West Indies

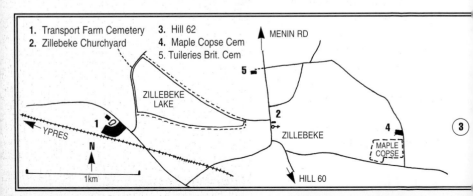

Regiment. Of the total 430 are unnamed, and including the above mentioned, there are 333 Special Memorials – mostly by the main entrance.

Outside of the main cemeteries like Tyne Cot and Lijessenthoek, one of the largest concentrations of Canadian graves in the Salient can be found here; men from several of the Canadian divisions killed holding the line at St Eloi, and in the Hill 62 – Observatory Ridge – Mount Sorrel – Hill 60 sectors during the first half of 1916. Lieutenant A.N.P.Service (VI-J-1) was killed by a shell in Trench 38 at Hill 60 on 18th August 1916. He was the brother of a famous Canadian poet, Robert Service, who himself served with the Canadian Army Medical Corps here in 1916 and later published *Rhymes of a Red Cross Man*. In Plot VI, Row I is a battalion burial site of men from the 60th Bn Canadian Infantry. Nineteen of them died on 12th August 1916 when the battalion was holding trenches 37 to 42 on Hill 60. At one point that day the Germans raided the front line positions, and carrying boxes of dynamite, succeeded in entering trenches 37, 39 and 41. However, men of the 60th soon beat them back and the boxes of dynamite and their fuses were captured and handed over to a RE tunnelling officer who was inspecting Hill 60 at the time. In the defence of these trenches the battalion lost two officers and twenty-six men killed, and two officers and fifty-six men wounded[1].

A number of other battalion, brigade or divisional burial sites can also be found at Transport Farm, including many soldiers who died in the fighting around Hill 60. The 1/4th Bn Yorkshire Regiment buried a number of their men in Plot II, Row K in early 1916. Twelve of them died on 14th February when the Germans blew a mine at trenches 37 and 38 south of the Ypres – Comines railway cutting between Hill 60 and Verbrandenmolen. A strong bombardment of the British positions followed in which many of the front line trenches, and communication trenches leading up to them, were damaged, destroyed or blown in. Contact was lost with the men in the forward positions and as the bombardment slackened, officers and men made their way back into the front line. Here '...two men were dug out alive from the trench near the crater and one

An entrance to a trench at Zillebeke Lake, c.1915.

man picked up alive after having been blown 40 yards...he died soon after he had been brought in.'[2] Also in Plot II is a mass grave of men from 8th Bn Durham Light Infantry. Fifteen graves in Row D are men who died on 2nd March 1916 when several units in the 17th (Northern) Division attacked the Bluff. 8th DLI were holding positions just north of Verbrandenmolen, and not directly involved in the attack, but came under tremendous punishment during the day. Apart from a heavy bombardment of shells of all calibres, phosgene gas descended on the Birdcage and a mine was blown[3].

From the fighting for Hill 60 during 1917 are several graves of interest. One is a group of officers from 11th Bn West Yorkshires Regiment. This was the battalion which actually captured the hill during the Battle of Messines on 7th June 1917, and six of their officers are buried in VII-N-5; the inscription on one of the headstones reads, 'To faithful warriors cometh rest'. The last Hill 60 Victoria Cross winner is buried here. Second Lieutenant F.Youens VC (I-O-3) of the 13th Bn DLI received the award posthumously on 7th July 1917 for bravery in the fighting from Hill 60 to Battle Wood. Lieutenant Colonel J.H.Bowes-Wilson (VII-M-10) is the most senior officer buried at Transport Farm and was killed commanding 9th Bn York and Lancaster Regiment on 7th June 1917, aged thirty-seven. His headstone bears the badge of his original regiment, the Duke of Wellingtons.

Leaving the cemetery by the main entrance, turn right onto the road and continue for a short distance then take the first turning on the left. This is the signposted entrance to Zillebeke Lake or Zillebeke Vijver. Stay on this and beyond the trees the lake is soon visible.

Two British soldiers survey Zillebeke Lake, 1917.

A howitzer being brought up to the fighting at Zillebeke in 1914.

Continue to the first building on the western edge of the lake; there is a good panoramic view from here.

Zillebeke Lake was known by several other names – Etang de Zillebeke or Zillebeke Bund among them – during the war. It was the only significant area of water on the battlefield, and as early as 1914 British soldiers bathed in it. The water was never fit to drink, however, and signs warned soldiers against this obviously tempting idea. The high banks that surround the lake were tunnelled into and dugouts and an ADS constructed by 1917. Nearby men of the Royal Field Artillery established their gun sites, and the path that follows the edge of the lake was used as a route to and from the trenches east of Zillebeke village. The 1/5th Bn Leicestershire Regiment knew this area in mid-1915.

> *The lake is triangular and entirely artificial, being surrounded by a broad causeway, 6 feet high, with a pathway along the top. On the western edge the ground falls away, leaving a bank some twenty feet high, in which were built the 'Lake dugouts' – the home of one of the support battalions. From the corner house to the trenches there were two routes, one by the south side of the lake, past Railway dugouts...and Manor Farm to Square Wood; the other...along the north side of the lake, where a trench cut into the causeway gave us cover from observation from Hill 60.*[4]

Stay on the road and at the north-west corner of the lake take a tarmac path on the right which follows the north bank into the village. It takes less than twenty minutes to walk into Zillebeke from here. However, further along stop at the north-east corner of the lake.

Panoramic view of the ruins of Zillebeke photographed in July 1916.

This area was known as Hell-blast Corner to the men who served here during the war, as troops and limbers going to and from the forward positions would often be observed by the Germans on the high ground between Hill 62 and Observatory Ridge, or Hill 60, and be shelled. There was also a large headquarters dugout at this point, used variously by gunners, sappers and infantry battalions and brigades. Sir John Glubb, known in later life as 'Glubb Pasha', came to Zillebeke as a young subaltern in the Royal Engineers in December 1915. 151st Brigade had their HQ here at that time, and it was one of his regular haunts, as related in his memoirs *Into Battle*.

Continue on the path into the village. It brings you out into the main street, Zillebeke Dorp. Stop.

Sir John Glubb recalled passing through Zillebeke in December 1915.

> *Every shattered fragment of a house is full of filth, old clothes, rags and bedding, left behind by the original inhabitants when they fled, and since used for sleeping on or torn up to dress wounds. Everything is soaked with rain, blood and dirt. Strewn around are thousands of half-empty jam or bully-beef tins, the contents putrefying, together with the remains of rations, scraps of bone and meat. There is no living thing visible but rats, big brown rats, who themselves are often mangy, and who barely trouble to get out of your way.[5]*

Turn right and go towards the church. The entrance to the churchyard is a little further up, just in front of the church itself. The British graves are in a Plot to the left.

ZILLEBEKE CHURCHYARD

There are thirty-two graves in what is very much akin to an English churchyard, constituting a somewhat rare burial ground in the Salient. Although there are several other ranks, the majority of the graves are officers from the British regular army that went to war in 1914 – from newly commissioned subalterns to long serving Lieutenant Colonels.

During First Ypres in November 1914, cavalry units were in action around Zillebeke and used the churchyard to bury the officers who fell at that time. A few others were added later and the last burials were from Canadian units in June 1916.

The officers buried here give a good cross section of the type of men who were commissioned into the regular army before 1914. Many leading public schools are represented. Several of the men are from titled and wealthy families. All had good connections, and through them the parents of Lieutenant J.H.G.L.Steere (F-1) were able to erect a private grave marker, rather than the normal Portland headstone, over the grave of their son. He died on 17th November 1914 while serving with 3rd Bn Grenadier Guards. Lieutenant Colonel A. de C.Scott (H-3) is the most senior officer; he was killed at Hill 60 on 5th May 1915 while commanding 1st Bn Cheshire Regiment.

One of the most fascinating characters buried in Zillebeke Churchyard, who like Steere, has his own private grave marker – a huge tomb – is Second Lieutenant Baron Alexis de Gunzburg (B-1). De Gunzburg was Russian by birth whose parents had a town house in Paris and a chateau outside the city. Born in Paris, he was educated at Eton and acquired a great love of England. By 1914 he was working in London and following the outbreak of war became a naturalised British citizen so he could join the army. Commissioned into the 11th Hussars in September 1914, he served during First Ypres attached to the Royal Horse Guards and 7th Cavalry Brigade as an Interpreter. He was killed near Zillebeke on 6th November 1914 while carrying a message for Lord Kavanagh, commanding the brigade, to Colonel Wilson of the RHG – who was also killed that day.

Return to Zillebeke Dorp and turn left to the road junction. Here turn left and follow the road round a corner as it goes out of the village. Take the first turning on the left, past a pedestrian crossing, and signposted for Maple Copse Cemetery. Continue for some

Zillebeke Churchyard: the grave of Lieutenant John Steere.

Canadian support line trenches near Hill 62.

distance – this was a route up to the front line during the war – and just past where the trees of Maple Copse begin on your left, turn left at another CWGC sign for the same cemetery, and follow a minor road, Schachteweide Str.

MAPLE COPSE CEMETERY

Maple Copse is believed to have acquired its name because of the trees planted here rather than a Canadian connection; although the Canadians were here in force by 1916. Close to the front line during the war, there are good views from this cemetery towards Hill 62 – the Canadian memorial can usually be seen – and Sanctuary Wood. To the right the ground rises to Observatory Ridge. An officer of the 1/5th Leicesters called Maple Copse in 1915 an 'isolated little wood with several dugouts in it' and burials of men killed in the front line on nearby Hill 62 began about this time. By 1916 there was an ADS in Maple Copse, which was particularly well used during the Canadian action in this sector in June. It was also during this period that many of the original graves were destroyed by shellfire. By 1918 the cemetery was closed due to battle damage and after the war only twenty-six of the 256 graves could be positively identified. The rest are commemorated by Special Memorials; headstones arranged within the cemetery in alphabetical order. Of the total buried here 114 are British

Maple Copse Cemetery 1919.

and 142 Canadian; of these forty are unknown.

Many of the Canadian graves are from units in the 4th (Canadian) Division who were posted here after arrival in France in August 1916. There are several 60th Bn casualties, including Captain Hon. A.T. Shaughnessy (D-11) who was killed on 6th June 1916, aged forty-four. The graves of tunnellers are also in evidence; both men from 175th Tunnelling Company RE in November 1915, and five miners of 2nd Canadian Tunnelling Company all of whom died on 15th February 1917.

Leaving the cemetery turn left and follow this often winding minor road. As the ground rises there are good views, on a clear day, towards the Menin Road and Hooge over to your right. Stop.

Somewhere to the left of the road nearer Zillebeke was a farm building known as Dormy House. Although in ruins, it was reinforced with concrete supports and artillery units used this as an observation post. It had similar views across the ground as you have from this position. This area during the war was very different, of course, and Huntley Gordon recalled one visit to the OP in mid-1917 whilst serving with 112th Bde RFA.

Here through a concrete slot I had my first long look through binoculars at the enemy trenches. The gunner subaltern on duty pointed out the various landmarks which were not easy to see in that monotonous landscape.

First there was the area of Sanctuary Wood; not really a wood, only a wilderness of splintered tree-stumps, and certainly no place to go for sanctuary...Then over to the left more skeleton trees, identified as Glencorse Wood, Inverness Copse and Blackwatch Corner... But don't think that these places could be identified by anyone but an expert. All I could see was lines and lines of sandbags alternating with hedges of rusty barbed wire, brown earth and grey splintered tree-trunks.[6]

Continue. After some time the road joins another from the right. Turn left and at the fork go right, along the street of a modern housing estate. This brings you out onto the main road from Zillebeke to the Menin Road, and a green CWGC signpost indicates a military cemetery opposite down a path between the houses.

TUILERIES BRITISH CEMETERY

The Tuileries was a tile factory west of the road that ran from Hell

Fire Corner on the Menin Road into Zillebeke village. The buildings were used widely during the war and, totally destroyed by 1918, the factory was never rebuilt. A small military burial ground was started nearby in 1915, and largely as a result of fighting near Hill 60, 106 British and three French soldiers were buried in what is now the cemetery. Subsequent fighting in this area damaged many of the grave markers and now the only identified graves are those in Plot I, of whom sixteen are unknowns. The remaining eighty are commemorated by Special Memorials which line the walls creating a huge open lawn in the middle and thereby making it unlike any other cemetery in the Salient.

Three battalions from the 5th Division dominate the burials: 1st Royal West Kents, 1st Cheshires and 2nd Duke of Wellingtons. Each has around twenty casualties buried at Tuileries from the period leading up to the heavy fighting on Hill 60 in May 1915. Captain J.E.G.Brown (A-2) died with 1st Bn Royal West Kent Regiment on 22nd February 1915 while serving as the battalion's scout and bombing officer. Brown had joined the army in 1911, was posted to 2nd Bn in India, and became a specialist in Indian languages, hoping to transfer to the Indian Army. But the war broke out and by October 1914 he was in the front line near Zillebeke; by Christmas he was an acting company commander.

Return via the path to the road and turn right. Go back into Zillebeke and turn right before the church down the same route you used to come from Zillebeke Lake earlier in the walk. It takes you back to Hell-blast Corner; this time follow the left hand path taking you round the southern edge of the lake. Eventually you will come to the main entrance for the lake and follow this back out onto the road. Go right, and Transport Farm Cemetery is a little further along on the left.

1 60th Bn Canadian Infantry *War Diary*, 12.8.16, PRO WO95/3879.
2 1/4th Bn Yorkshire Regiment *War Diary*, 14.2.16, PRO WO95/2836.
3 8th Bn Durham Light Infantry *War Diary*, 2.3.16, PRO WO95/2841.
4 Hills, J.D. *The Fifth Leicestershire: A Record of the 1/5th Battalion the Leicestershire Regiment TF during the War* 1914-1919 (Echo Press 1919) p.41.
5 Glubb, J. *Into Battle: A Soldier's Diary of the Great War* (Cassell 1978) p.28.
6 Gordon, H. *The Unreturning Army: A Field Gunner in Flanders 1917-18* (J.M.Dent 1967) p.41-42.

A knocked out British tank near Zillebeke in 1919.

Chapter Five

THE BLUFF – HILL 60 WALK

STARTING POINT: **Bedford House Cemetery.**
DURATION: **5 hours (excluding time on Hill 60).**

WALK SUMMARY: *A long but rewarding walk, largely along quiet tracks or minor roads, taking you across the Bluff to the infamous Hill 60. Several front line cemeteries are visited en-route.*

Park your vehicle either outside the entrance to Bedford House Cemetery in a lay-by or, if the gates are open, follow the drive down and park at the end.

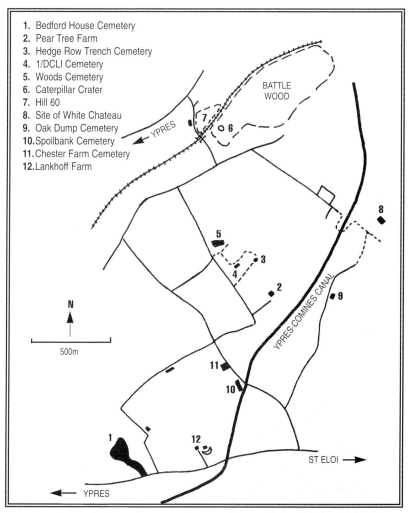

1. Bedford House Cemetery
2. Pear Tree Farm
3. Hedge Row Trench Cemetery
4. 1/DCLI Cemetery
5. Woods Cemetery
6. Caterpillar Crater
7. Hill 60
8. Site of White Chateau
9. Oak Dump Cemetery
10. Spoilbank Cemetery
11. Chester Farm Cemetery
12. Lankhoff Farm

BATTLE WOOD

YPRES

N

500m

YPRES-COMINES CANAL

ST ELOI →

← YPRES

BEDFORD HOUSE CEMETERY

One of the larger cemeteries in the Salient, it is situated in the grounds of the old chateau Rosendal, called Bedford House or Woodcote House on British maps. It remained behind the British lines for the whole of the war, and the chateau buildings were gradually destroyed by shellfire. The cellars and outbuildings were used as an Advanced Dressing Station (ADS) by RAMC Field Ambulances, and the main house as a brigade headquarters. By the Armistice there were six so-called 'enclosures', Numbers 1 and 5 being removed to other cemeteries in the 1920s. The three remaining ones became Bedford House Cemetery and a sixth, forgotten enclosure, was later discovered and this is now by the main entrance, where there are also a number of Second World War graves. Canon Scot, serving as a chaplain with 1st (Canadian) Division, visited Bedford House in April 1916.

Bedford House... stood in what must have been once very beautiful grounds. The upper part of the house was in ruins, but the cellars were deep and capacious and formed a good billet for the officers and men. At one side there was a dressing station and in the garden were some huts protected by piles of sandbags.[1]

An original photograph of a grave in Bedford House Cemetery: Pte A.E.Kemp of the 1/19th Londons.

In total there are 5,067 burials at Bedford House, of which some sixty percent are unknowns. It is best to examine each of the enclosures individually.

Enclosure No 2 was started in December 1915, and remained in use until October 1918. Post-war 437 graves were added, the majority of which came from the Ecole de Bienfaisance and Asylum British cemeteries in Ypres. The former was located on the south side of the Menin road, just north of the railway line, in the grounds of a large school which served as an ADS. By 1918 there were 140 graves. Asylum British Cemetery was the largest concentrated into Bedford House,

82

with 283 burials. Located alongside a large mental hospital just outside Ypres on the Poperinghe road, it also served as an ADS and was used from 1915-17. The total number of graves in Enclosure No 2 is therefore: 672 British, twenty-two Australian, twenty-one Canadian, five New Zealand, five British West Indies and one German flying officer. Of these thirty-three are unknown and there are twenty-four Special Memorials.

Among the soldiers here are a large number of Hooge casualties, particularly from units in the 14th (Light) Division. Elsewhere, Lieutenant Colonel O.M.Croshaw DSO (I-A-21) was an officer in the Glasgow Yeomanry who died commanding 53rd Bn Australian Infantry on 26th September 1917. The Australian official historian, C.E.W.Bean, felt that Croshaw was 'one of the noblest British officers in the AIF' and records that he had a premonition of his death saying to his fellow officers before the attack on Polygon Wood, 'Gentlemen, your men before yourselves. Look to your flanks. God bless you lads, till we meet again.'[2]

Enclosure No 3 is the smallest at Bedford House, used only for a limited time between February 1915 and December 1916. There are fifty-five British and five Canadian graves; of the former, twenty-two are men of the 7th Bn East Yorkshire Regiment killed between August and October 1915. No additional burials were moved in here after the war.

Enclosure No 4 is the largest with 3,188 British burials, 309 Canadian, 179 Australian, twenty-five New Zealand, twenty Indian, seventeen South African, three Royal Guernsey Light Infantry, one British West Indies, one Russian and one German. Of these 2,478 are unknown and there are twenty-five Special Memorials. This enclosure was started in June 1916 and continued in use until February 1918. The original graves were largely men from London Regiment battalions of the 47th (London) Division, including a row of London Irish Riflemen in Plot I, Row I, who died in a trench raid on the German lines at Verbrandenmolen in April 1917. After the war 3,324 burials were moved in here, many from former German burial grounds which contained British casualties.

Captain G.F.H.Charlton (XIII-H-5) was killed on 6th October 1916 with 10th Bn South Wales Borderers. The register records that 'his only brother fell near Warlencourt, Somme, 26th August 1918'. A senior officer is Lieutenant Colonel G.S.Tulloch (XI-C-11), a Boer War veteran who died commanding 2nd Bn Gloucestershire Regiment at Sanctuary Wood on 9th May 1915, aged forty-eight. Two brothers are buried here. Privates G.Hamilton (I-P-3) and S.Hamilton (I-K-12) were both serving with the 21st Bn Canadian Infantry near Mount Sorrel when they died on 14th June 1916. One of the most visited graves is that of Second Lieutenant R.P.Hallowes VC MC (XIV-B-36), 4th Bn Middlesex Regiment, who was mortally wounded at Hooge and died on 30th September 1915 (See Bellewaarde Ridge Walk).

Enclosure No 6 by the main entrance has 534 burials, of which 499 are unknowns. Records seem to indicate that after the war it was planned to move these graves elsewhere, as it was not included in the original cemetery register. A group of Second World War graves can be found here; men who largely died in the fighting near Hollebeke in May 1940.

Leave the cemetery by the driveway and gate, then turn left on the footpath by the main road and follow it for a short distance. Take the next turning on the left, Waastensestraat, and follow it right then left when a farm is reached. Continue, and as the road bends to the right, stop.

Ahead of you is a clear view of the ground known to British troops as the Bluff. The Ypres – Comines canal runs south from Ypres and at this point a large cutting was made across ground that is part of the Messines Ridge. The spoil from the excavations was thrown up either side of the canal, and it was this that was known as the Bluff, and further along, as Spoilbank. To your extreme left the modern wind propeller close to Hill 60 can be seen on clear days; ahead of you several Crosses of Sacrifice from military cemeteries can also be seen – this is Verbrandenmolen; and the wooded area on the right is the Bluff itself.

Trench lines were established in the area between Verbrandenmolen and the Bluff at the end of 1914 by French troops. The front line positions here when the British took over were all numbered, rather than named, trenches, and fighting continued for almost four years, the

The Bluff in 1915.

positions only moving a matter of a few yards here and there. Many units passed through this sector; 2nd Bn Manchester Regiment holds the record for the longest tour of duty. From April to July 1915 they held the Bluff for eighty-seven consecutive days. In February 1916 the Germans launched a series of attacks on the line then held by 14th (Light) Division, capturing at one point part of the British front line. Units of 3rd Division were called up and retook the trenches on 2nd March. A good account of the type of fighting during this action is given by Lieutenant Colonel H. d'Arch Smith of 2nd Bn Suffolk Regiment.

Zero hour was 4.30 and no preliminary bombardment warned the enemy; the advance moved silently forward and took them unaware. At 4.35 the Boche rockets went up, and a triple barrage fell across our line of attack; but he was too late; his first line trenches were in our hands before his gunners received the SOS. Our men advanced as the sticky ground would allow, and the objective was reached without much resistance except for a stubborn defence on the left which held up our men and caused many casualties before... they reached their aim. On the right the line of attack had to go round the lip of an enormous crater at the eastern end of the Bluff... As the day broke large streams of fleeing Huns could be seen inside our lines anxious to give themselves up, and striving to get under cover from the terrible rifle fire and bombardment from their own guns, which had now reached such a point of frenzy that you could not hear a word shouted close to your ear... The brilliant success of the attack was followed by the fearful work of consolidating, which in this case meant that you crouched behind a half blown away parapet and endeavoured to make it higher by filling sandbags with mud from under your own feet, piling these on top, and incidentally making a pond for your own feet to stand in... When finally the battalion was relieved, it took a whole long night, owing to the havoc of the ground.[3]

Mine warfare then became a very prominent feature of day to day life here, and many craters scarred the ridge between Verbrandenmolen and the Bluff. During the Battle of Messines in June 1917 this ground was captured. Passing to the Germans in April 1918, the final battle for the Bluff took place on 28th September 1918 when the 14th (Light) Division, who had been here in 1916, returned and swept up the position.

German front line trench at Verbrandenmolen. (Klaus Späth)

Continue on this road. Passing another farm, the road eventually meets another. Go straight across up a minor road, Verbrandenmolenstraat, also signposted with a CWGC board. This area is slowly being forested by the local council, with the intention of making a park. The trees already planted here are quick growing, and it is therefore likely that the landscape will change somewhat in the next few years. Stay on this minor road and follow it left further up. Go past a turning to the right – which leads to a farm known as Pear Tree Farm on trench maps – and a few hundred yards further on take the first track on the right. Follow this past the first track on the left, and continue uphill to a grassed area where the military cemetery is.

HEDGE ROW TRENCH CEMETERY

This cemetery, located close to the front line, was started in March 1915 when Private W.Drury (Sp Mem C-13) of the 2nd Duke of Wellingtons was killed and buried here on 24th March. It took its name from a nearby communication trench which ran up to the front line at Trench 32. Occasionally it was also known as Ravine Wood Cemetery. Graves were added, although they often suffered from shellfire, until August 1917. The burials consist of ninety-four British, two Canadian, and two whose names and units are unknown. Private W.A.Stokes (Sp Mem E-3) of the 3rd Bn Rifle Brigade is the youngest soldier here; he was only seventeen when he died on 29th October 1915. There is a significant representation of men from the 8th Buffs who died in November 1915, and the London Regiment from 1917; among the latter Captain H.W.Joel (Sp Mem D-3) of the First Surrey Rifles who was killed in the Battle of Messines on 7th June 1917, aged only twenty.

Leave by the gate and go straight down a grassed avenue between some young trees. Following the curve of silver birch trees on your right, you will come out to the next cemetery.

1/DCLI CEMETERY, THE BLUFF

Named after, and started by, 1st Bn Duke of Cornwall's Light Infantry in April 1915, the unit buried their dead in this cemetery until July. Fifty-one officers and men from this battalion rest here, and a few from other regiments were added afterwards. In 1919 twenty-three graves were moved in from the area between Hill 60 and the Bluff, and now form Row D.

An interesting headstone is found among the unknown graves in Row D. It reads, 'A Captain of the Great War, Queen Victoria's Rifles'. The Queen Victoria's Rifles (QVRs) were the 9th Bn London Regiment and in April 1915 were in action on Hill 60. This grave and other unknowns from the QVRs buried here presumably relate to this action as the battalion was never in this part of the Salient again for the rest of the war. Research has shown that only one Captain from the QVRs died at this time and has no known grave, his name being recorded on the Menin Gate. He is Captain Gilbert Fazakerley-Westby who was killed on 21st April 1915. Born at Grosvenor Square in 1881, his parents lived in Mowbreck Hall, Kirkham, and he joined the QVRs in 1911, crossing to France with them in November 1914. After his death at Hill 60 the QVRs commanding officer wrote, '... I cannot speak too highly of your son; all ranks loved and respected him. His fortitude and forbearance during that terrible week [at Hill 60] was an example to the whole regiment and never to be forgotten.' It seems most likely that this is Fazakerley-Westby's grave, although enquiries with the CWGC have so far proved fruitless.

Leaving the cemetery, turn left and follow the cut grass path prepared by the CWGC, which leads to the next cemetery.

WOODS CEMETERY

The cemetery was started by 1st Dorsets and 1st East Surreys in April 1915, and remained in use until September 1917. Close to the trenches, men killed in the front line were brought back here for burial by units serving in this sector. Canadian and London Regiment graves are particularly numerous. There are 212 British burials, 111 Canadian and three Australian. Of these thirty-two are unknown.

The Canadian graves largely date from April 1916, and are men from units in the 1st (Canadian) Division. Private F.E.Calderon (II-G-11) of 2nd Bn Canadian Infantry was killed on 3rd April 1916, aged forty-two. His father was a member of the Royal Academy, and Calderon himself was born in London, educated at Rugby and worked in the Maritime department of Canada between 1907 and 1914. Elsewhere, London Regiment graves are from battalions in the 47th (London) Division who occupied this sector from late 1916 onwards, when they arrived here after several engagements on the Somme (most notably High Wood), until after the Battle of Messines. The first of their burials are found in Plots IV and V; among the early casualties was S.H.Moxon (V-B-2) who has the unusual rank of Sergeant-Bugler. An accomplished musician, he died on 25th October 1916, aged thirty-eight, and was a King's Trumpeter and member of the Royal Society of Musicians.

A unique aspect of this cemetery is a field grave that forms a promontory on the western wall (II-Z-1). Possibly a shell hole or gun pit, these three men of the Royal Artillery lie where they were buried by their comrades in 1917. The date of death is recorded as 12th November; two are shown as belonging to 124th Brigade RFA and the other Y/37 Trench Mortar Battery. It is likely all three died while manning a 2-inch heavy trench mortar, better known as a 'Toffee Apple', or 'Plum Pudding', as these weapons operated very close to the front line.

Leave the cemetery by the grass path until it meets a metalled track. Turn right and follow to the end where it joins the main Ypres – Hollebeke road. Turn right, keeping to the right, continue past a turning to the right, and then just a little further along on the left is another turning signposted for Hill 60. Before taking this route, stop and look across the fields to the right of the road.

This was the area where the front line trenches ran south from the Caterpillar and Hill 60 onto Verbrandenmolen and the Bluff. Trenches 34, 35 and 36 were here, often known as 'Bomb Corner'. A good description of this sector in 1915 is given by the 1/5th Bn Leicestershire Regiment.

The lines at this time were very close together, and at one point... less than 50 yards separated our parapet from the Boche's... One's parapet in this area was one's trench, for digging was impossible, and we lived behind a sort of glorified sandbag grouse butt, six feet thick at the base and two to three feet at the top, sometimes, but not always, bullet-proof.

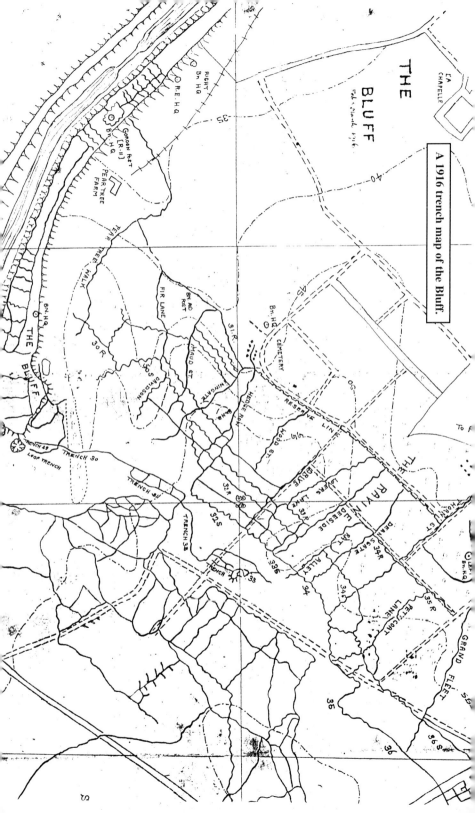

A 1916 trench map of the Bluff.

One or two amusing stories are told about the infantry opposite '35', who were Saxons, and inclined to be friendly with the English. On one occasion the following message, tied to a stone, was thrown into our trench: 'We are going to send a 40lb bomb. We have got to do it, but we don't want to. I will come this evening, and we will whistle first to warn you.' All of this happened.'[4]

Now follow the road on the left, signposted for Hill 60. Just before the railway bridge visible ahead of you, stop, and look across the fields on your right towards the wooded area.

You are looking at the ground in front of a position known as the caterpillar on British maps. For most of the war the British lines were just in front of the road, with the German trenches by the tree line. The main British line was Trench 37, and just before Second Ypres in April 1915, the machine-gun section of 9th Londons (Queen Victoria's Rifles) set up here and fired on the German positions on Hill 60 itself. For the Battle of Messines, the Caterpillar was selected as a target for one of the offensive mines. Started by 3rd Canadian Tunnelling Company in 1916, after some six months it was taken over by 1st Australian Tunnelling Company and eventually fired at 3.10am on 7th June 1917. A charge of 70,000lbs of Ammonal was used, forming a crater 275 feet wide and sixty feet deep, enabling the men of 23rd Division to capture the ground at minimal cost. Unfortunately this impressive crater is on private land and cannot be visited.

Continue across the bridge.

HILL 60 was the centrepiece of the fighting at Ypres, in particular during the first half of 1915. An artificial hill, sixty metres above sea level (thus its name), it was created from the spoil when the railway cutting was dug in the nineteenth century. Known as 'Lover's Knoll'

The railway cutting and bridge at Hill 60 looking towards Trench 38, 1915.

Modern aerial view of Hill 60. (John Giles)

before the war, as it was a favourite haunt of courting couples, it later took on somewhat more ominous tones. The French occupied the hill in 1914, the British taking over in February 1915. Mine warfare had already begun at Hill 60 when the French miner Lieutenant Bruyeat began offensive operations against the German positions on the crest. At this stage in the war no proper Tunnelling Companies existed in the British army and men of the Monmouthshire Regiment carried on from where Bruyeat had left off. It was not until the spring of 1915 that a group of engineers from the newly formed 171st Tunnelling Company,

under the inspiration of Major Norton Griffiths, blew a mine on 17th April to assist the 5th Division's attack on Hill 60. During these operations four Victoria Crosses were won on the hill; by Second Lieutenant Harold Woolley of the QVRs (the first territorial to win the VC), and three men of the 1st Bn East Surrey Regiment: Private E.Dwyer, Second Lieutenant B.Geary, and Lieutenant G.Roupel. Possession of the hill passed to the Germans on 5th May

L/Cpl E.Dwyer VC (right) photographed in England, August 1915.

1915 and it remained in their hands until the Battle of Messines in 1917. Mine warfare continued on both sides so that by 1916 No Man's Land directly below the hill was one long line of mine craters.

Meanwhile the German line was reinforced with concrete bunkers and it became clear that a full frontal attack on Hill 60 would be suicidal. As part of the Messines mining operations, Hill 60 became the northern-most target on the Messines Ridge. 3rd Canadian Tunnelling Company prepared a mine that was handed over to 1st Australian Tunnelling Company, as at the Caterpillar. A charge of 53,000lbs of Ammonal and gun cotton blew a chunk out of the right-hand sector of the hill, neutralising what was left of the German garrison and enabling men of the 11th Bn West Yorkshire Regiment to take the position. A German account recorded,

> '... the ground trembled as in a natural earthquake, heavy concrete shelters rocked, a hurricane of hot air from the explosions swept back for many kilometres, dropping fragments of wood, iron and earth; and gigantic black clouds of smoke and dust spread over the country. The effect on the troops was overpowering and crushing.'[5]

Following the capture of Hill 60, the front lines were further along the railway line at Battle Wood, near Hollebeke. Re-taken by the Germans in April 1918, Hill 60 returned to British hands without a fight in September 1918.

Today Hill 60 is one of the few British sectors of the Western Front to be preserved in its 1918 state. It is a large site and the whole hill can be reached on foot, requiring at least an hour including all the memorials, bunkers and nearby café/museum. Nearest to the railway bridge is the memorial to the 14th (Light) Division, moved here from Railway Wood in 1978. Nearby is the 1st Australian Tunnelling Company memorial and, just past it, access to the hill itself is gained by a gate. The path takes you down into what seems like a natural gully; this is in fact the crater zone from all the mine explosions which took place here during 1915-16. On the crest is evidence of German concrete bunkers, the 1917 mine crater and a memorial to Harold Woolley's Queen Victoria's Rifles. The latter is a replacement of the original which was destroyed during the fighting in May 1940.

The original QVR memorial on Hill 60.

Sign on building: "NO MAN'S LAND CANTEEN" HILL 60 / RUN BY BRITISH EX-SERVICE MEN

'No Man's Land Canteen': many ex-servicemen stayed on after the war:
one opened a canteen on Hill 60 that served pilgrims in the 1920s.

On the Battle Wood side is a rare example of a British bunker, this one
constructed by Australian Engineers in 1918, and used as an
observation post overlooking Hollebeke. Returning to the road via the
QVR memorial, opposite the hill is a café which has a small collection
of militaria relating to the fighting on Hill 60. Those used to museums
in Ypres and at Hooge might find it a little disappointing as the exhibits
are arranged in a somewhat haphazard fashion. It nevertheless serves
as a useful refreshment stop.

Return to the Hollebeke road by re-crossing the railway bridge
and where this road meets the main road, turn left. After a short walk,
take the first road on the right, signposted for Palingbeek, and tree-
lined all the way to another café, car park and a wooded area by the
canal.

When you reach the woodland you are on the area of the Bluff itself.
Although now a nature reserve, signs of the war are never very far
away among the trees. This is a popular local attraction for the people
of Ypres, a setting now a world away from the horror which unfolded
here during the war years. An officer in the 7th Bn York and Lancasters
recalls a typical episode in February 1916 after the Germans had blown
a mine.

*I saw the Bluff... and it presented a haunting spectacle. Upon
the slopes of the crater were the dead, frozen as they had been*

93

killed, for the weather was intensely cold... Silhouetted against the skyline, and plainly visible from the British line, was the figure of the only man who had looked upon the invisible enemy. Clad in his great coat, his shrapnel helmet was still on his head. His right knee was bent to the ground; his right hand grasped the barrel of his rifle, the butt of which also rested in the ground. He had been frozen stiff as he had died; turned into a terribly arresting sculpture by the frost.[6]

German front line bunker on Hill 60, 1916.
(Klaus Späth)

Captured in June 1917, the Bluff remained in British hands until April 1918 when German troops captured it during the Spring Offensive. At that time it was held by the 13th Bn Royal Sussex Regiment (3rd South Downs) whose front line companies, well under strength following heavy casualties on the Somme in March, were quickly wiped out. The defence of the Bluff passed to the battalion headquarters, led by the commanding officer Lieutenant Colonel H.T.K.Robinson DSO, a veteran who had served in France since 1916. He roused his staff, cooks and stretcher-bearers and anyone he could find for a final stand at his HQ dugout. They fought to the last man and were overwhelmed by sheer weight of numbers. Robinson and many of his scratch mob were killed; none have graves and are commemorated on the Tyne Cot Memorial.

Follow wooden steps down to the canal and cross it by a small **The railway cutting and bridge at Hill 60, 1915.**

bridge. Further steps will take you up the other side and eventually out onto a metalled track just south of the Bluff. Follow this to where another joins it from the right. Stop.

Ahead of you in the trees was the wartime location of White Chateau. This was a large ornate house, in ruins by 1917, forming part of the German second line south of the Ypres – Comines canal between Oak Support and Oak Reserve trenches. For the Battle of Messines on 7th June 1917, the 140th Brigade of 47th (London) Division attacked here with the aid of four tanks. The 7th and 8th Bns of the London Regiment captured the German front line, but were held up by a determined garrison holed up in the chateau grounds. This was cleared when a party led by Lieutenant J.F.Preston from 7th Londons stormed the rubble and White Chateau was taken. In the fighting 140th Brigade captured 282 prisoners, and lost forty officers and 956 men.

Take the minor road on the right, and continue until a military cemetery is reached on the left.

OAK DUMP CEMETERY

This small battlefield cemetery was started during the Messines offensive in June 1917 by units of the 47th (London) Division who captured this ground. Of the 109 British graves, fifty-nine are soldiers of the London Regiment. There are also two Australians, and of the total five are unknown. The bodies of seven men of 180th Siege Battery RGA, who were killed near White Chateau in March 1918, were found in 1927 and moved to this cemetery.

Return to the road and turn left following it to the end where it joins another. Turn right, back towards the canal. Cross the bridge over the canal and there are two military cemeteries a short distance apart on the left of the road.

SPOILBANK CEMETERY

This cemetery takes its name from the nearby banks of spoil alongside the Ypres – Comines canal known to the British as Spoilbank. It was also known as Gordon Terrace Cemetery and was started in February 1915, remaining in use until March 1918. Spoilbank Cemetery is particularly associated with the 2nd Bn Suffolk Regiment, who were on the Bluff in early 1916, and a row of their dead can be found in Plot I, Row B. After the war 116 graves were moved in from a wide area around Ypres. The total burials here are: 426 British, sixty-seven Australian, and sixteen Canadian. Of these 125 are unknowns, and there are eleven Special Memorials.

Among the Special Memorials are an officer and six gunners of 298th Army Brigade RFA. Second Lieutenant H.C.Rowe (Sp Mem B-6) and his men had their guns alongside the canal at Lock 8, north of Convent Lane, when on 19th July 1917 they were killed by shell fire while working on a new battery position[7].

Three officers from the headquarters of 10th Bn Royal Welsh Fusiliers are also buried here: Lieutenant Colonel S.S.Binney DSO (I-M-4), Major E.Freeman (I-M-5) and Captain & Adjutant W.T.Lyons (I-M-3). On 3rd March 1916, '... a shell of large calibre made a direct hit on Battalion Headquarters in Gordon Post, killing the Commanding Officer, Second in Command and Adjutant.'[8] Binney was a regular army officer who had previously fought with the XIXth Hussars in the Boer War, winning the Distinguished Service Order. He latterly served on the Staff at Sandhurst and had retired when war broke out. In 1914 he was recalled and served as a Railway Transport Officer, becoming Deputy Director of Railway Transport in France. Promoted to Lieutenant Colonel, he went to command 10th Royal Welsh in February 1916, a post he held for only a matter of weeks.

Two brothers are buried side by side here. Second Lieutenant G.Keating (I-H-3) and Lieutenant J.Keating (I-H-4), both of 2nd Bn Cheshire Regiment, died on 17th February 1915. On this day their battalion made a two company attack, from Chester Farm towards the Bluff, which was '... checked by hostile machine-guns which opened up at short range.'[9] Long serving regular soldiers with over twenty years service each, they had been commissioned from the ranks in 1914. It is believed they were killed by the same burst of machine-gun fire.

CHESTER FARM CEMETERY

Named after a farm which is almost opposite the cemetery, itself probably named by the 2nd Cheshires in 1915, the cemetery was started in March 1915 and used by front line units on the Bluff and Verbrandenmolen until November 1917. Many graves are grouped by regiment and battalion; for example there are ninety-two men of the 2nd Bn Manchester Regiment who were killed between April and July 1915 buried in Plot I. In various parts of the cemetery are seventy-two officers and men from battalions of the London Regiment. In total there are 306 British graves, eighty-seven Canadian, twenty-one Australian, and four German prisoners.

The first two burials are soldiers from 1st Bn Norfolk Regiment. Privates W.Barnes (II-AA-1A) and O.Taylor (II-AA-1) were killed on

15th March 1915. Later graves include two young soldiers, both seventeen: Private H.Bagshaw (I-B-5) of 1/6th Bn Sherwood Foresters who died on 21st September 1915, and Rifleman E.E.G.Miles (I-K-33), London Irish Rifles, killed 12th June 1917. Lieutenant E.S.Carlos (I-K-36) was a talented artist killed here during the Battle of Messines on 14th June 1917 whilst serving with the 8th Buffs.

Return towards the canal bridge, and just before it turn right, following a towpath. Continue until it brings you to the main Ypres – Armentieres road. Opposite is a Demarcation Stone. Cross the road carefully to see it.

This Demarcation Stone marks the closest the Germans got to the southern side of Ypres in April 1918. The Bluff and other positions on the Messines Ridge, captured in 1917, were lost in a matter of days, but the line of the Ypres – Comines canal formed a natural barrier at this point and it was here the Germans were slowed down and stopped, largely by the 7th Bn Leicestershire Regiment. Bedford House and Lankhof Farm (see below) then became part of the front line.

Re-cross the road and follow the footpath in the direction of Ypres. Further along on the right some concrete bunkers by a farm, set back from the road, can be seen.

The buildings behind were known as Lankhof Farm on British maps, and the bunkers took this name. Constructed around 1916, they were used at various times as brigade and battalion headquarters, and also by the many artillery units which had their gun sites in the fields close by. They are on private land, and access is only gained by permission of the farmer.

Continue along this road, which will shortly bring you back to Bedford House Cemetery and your vehicle.

1 Scott, F.G. *The Great War As I Saw It* (Goodchild 1922) p.126.
2 Bean, C.E.W. *The AIF In France 1917* (Angus & Robertson 1933) p.827.
3 Quoted in Brice, B. *The Battle Book of Ypres* (John Murray 1927) p.61-62.
4 Hills, J.D. *The Fifth Leicestershire: A Record of the 1/5th Battalion the Leicestershire Regiment 1F during the War 1914-1919* (Echo Press 1919) p.45-47.
5 Edmonds, J.E. *Military Operations France and Belgium 1917 Volume II* (HMSO 1948) p.61.
6 Brice op cit. p.60.
7 298th Army Brigade RFA *War Diary*, 19.7.17, PRO WO95/456.
8 10th Bn Royal Welsh Fusiliers *War Diary*, 3.3.16, PRO WO95/1436.
9 2nd Bn Cheshire Regiment *War Diary*, 17.2.15, PRO WO95/2276.

Counting down the minutes: a contemporary illustration showing a tunnelling officer waiting for Zero Hour on 7th June 1917.

Chapter Six

PASSCHENDAELE WALK

STARTING POINT: **Tyne Cot Cemetery.**
DURATION: **2 hours.**

WALK SUMMARY: *A short walk for those either with little time or who are inexperienced walkers, taking in the valley before Passchendaele where the last attacks on the village took place during Third Ypres in 1917.*

Leave your vehicle outside Tyne Cot Cemetery. Although it can be busy here, especially in the summer months, there is usually somewhere to park. Enter the cemetery by the main gate.

TYNE COT CEMETERY & MEMORIAL

Tyne Cot is the largest British military cemetery in the world, from either world war, with 11,908 graves. It is also the most visited; visitors are found here on every day of the year and by the summer months lines of cars and coaches almost block out the entrance. It is often used by school parties to give their students an impression of the scale of losses suffered by all sides in the Great War, and although many find it impressive, some feel the sheer numbers make a visit here impersonal – there are simply too many graves to take in.

Tyne Cot, or Cottages, was the name given to a small collection of Flemish buildings on the Broodseinde Ridge. The origins of this name have long been in dispute; the most commonly accepted story is that it arose from the involvement of the 50th (Northumbrian) Division in this area during Third Ypres, but it was marked on British maps as Tyne

TAYLOR LIBRARY

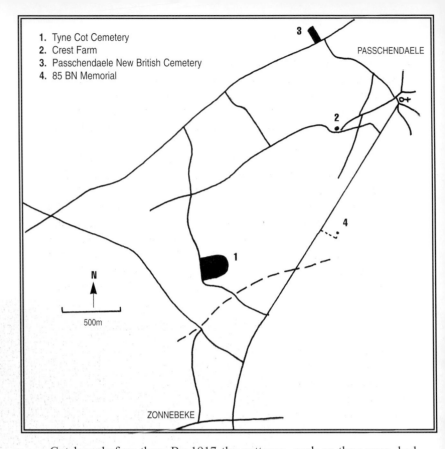

1. Tyne Cot Cemetery
2. Crest Farm
3. Passchendaele New British Cemetery
4. 85 BN Memorial

PASSCHENDAELE

N

500m

ZONNEBEKE

Cot long before then. By 1917 the cottages, such as they were, had gone – blasted by British shellfire. The area had been reinforced, as elsewhere on the Passchendaele Battlefield, with a complex of German concrete bunkers. Four of them were at Tyne Cot, with a command bunker, and machine-gun positions with inter-locking fields of fire; three are now preserved within the confines of the cemetery. Standing here today the view afforded from this position is obvious. Even on a misty day the spires of Ypres are visible; the ground attacked over and captured by the Australians in October 1917 was clearly dominated by this low ridge – the Broodseinde Ridge. The original graves, found behind the Cross of Sacrifice, date from November 1917 to February 1918 when the command bunker (now under the Cross) was used as a regimental aid post. Those who died of wounds were buried in shell holes nearby, including several German prisoners, and this explains the random nature of these burials.

As early as 1919 the Imperial War Graves Commission selected this site to construct a main Ypres battlefield cemetery; concentrating graves from all over the Salient. The movement of over 11,000 bodies, a mammoth task, was not completed until 1922, when King George V came to see what was then a hillside of wooden crosses. As part of his tour some steps had been placed against the command bunker; from the top were some excellent views across the ground here. He suggested that this feature should be incorporated into the final cemetery and today there are steps up the side of the Cross allowing access to the top – although they are very steep and care should be taken. Work to make the cemetery permanent began after the King's visit, and Herbert Baker designed the layout and design of both the main cemetery and the eventual memorial to the missing. A friend and colleague of Edwin Lutyens, Baker also worked on the memorials at Neuve Chapelle, Loos and Delville Wood. Tyne Cot was completed within five years and it was officially opened on 19th June 1927.

The burials at Tyne Cot Cemetery are arranged in sixty-seven plots and total:

British	8,953
Australian	1,368
Canadian	966
New Zealand	520
South African	90
Newfoundland	14
Channel Islands	6
German	4
West Indies	2
French	1

Tyne Cot Cemetery in the 1920's – a photograph taken from the command bunker.

Of this number 8,366 are unknowns; seventy percent of the total.

Those buried here represent a myriad of units, of actions, battles and engagements large, small, forgotten or much lauded. Casualties from all four battles of Ypres can be found, and there are three Victoria Cross winners:

Captain C.S.Jeffries VC (XL-E-1)
- 34th Bn AIF, killed 12th October 1917.
Sgt L.McGee VC (XX-D-1)
 - 40th Bn AIF, killed 13th October 1917.
Pte J.P.Robertson VC (LVIII-D-26)
- 27th Bn Canadian Infantry, killed 6th November 1917.

Among the others are many interesting characters who are often overlooked by the summer visitors. H.Barries (Sp Mem 60) was a Piper in the 1st Bn Cameron Highlanders, killed while piping his comrades forward on 5th November 1914. RSM C.F.Jagger (XVI-A-5) of 1/4th Bn East Yorkshire Regiment died on 13th December 1917. He was among that rare breed of soldier – a Warrant Officer who was awarded the Military Cross. Royal Flying Corps graves are numerous, particularly in Plot I, Row AA, where two eighteen-year-old pilots are buried. Elsewhere is Captain V.N.H.Wadham (LXII-C-5), a veteran RFC officer. Killed on 17th January 1916, the register records he was 'one of the 34 pilots who flew from Salisbury Plain to France on 12th August 1914'. The two most senior officers at Tyne Cot are Brigadier-General J.F.Riddell (XXXIV-H-14), a Northumberland Fusiliers officer who was killed in action commanding 1/1st Northumberland Brigade near St Julien on 26th April 1915, aged fifty-two. Lieutenant Colonel S.H.Dix MC (XLVI-B-1) was the commanding officer of 12th/13th Northumberland Fusiliers, and fell at Passchendaele on 4th October 1917, aged thirty-nine.

Reading the inscriptions on headstones at Tyne Cot gives a good impression of how the families of these men viewed the sacrifice of their loved ones in the post war world. There are references to Country, Empire and God. Today most modern pilgrims are inclined to write 'why?' in the cemetery visitors' book, but the grave of Second Lieutenant A.C.Young (IV-G-21) bears one of the very few anti-war inscriptions to be found anywhere on the Western Front battlefields. Commissioned into the 7/8th Royal Irish Fusiliers, Young was a veteran of the Somme. He was killed near the Steenbeek on 16th August 1917, aged twenty-six. The son of a diplomat who had served in Japan for most of his career, Young's father was moved to write 'sacrificed to the fallacy that war can end war'.

The Broodseinde Ridge in 1917.

The TYNE COT MEMORIAL forms the large arched wall to the rear of the cemetery. This takes over from where the Menin Gate leaves off, and commemorates those killed at Ypres from 16th August 1917 to the end of the war. The majority of names are men who died during Third Ypres and the German offensive in April 1918. The memorial records 34,927 soldiers; aside from British names, 1,176 are New Zealand and one Newfoundland. Australian, Canadian and South African 'missing' are on the Menin Gate. Arranged regimentally, the names are engraved on low stone walls. Among the casualties are three VC winners from Third Ypres:

Lieutenant Colonel P.E.Bent (Panel 50)
9th Bn Leicestershire Regiment, killed 1st October 1917.
Corporal W.Clamp (Panel 52)
6th Bn Yorkshire Regiment, killed 9th October 1917.
Corporal E.Seaman (Panel 70)
2nd Bn Royal Inniskilling Fusiliers, killed 29th September 1917.

Others of interest include:

A LIFE WITH HORSES: Charles Eddy was born in Bath, Somerset, and joined the regular army in the last few years of the nineteenth century. He was posted to the Hussars, with whom he served in the Boer War, and discovering a particular skill with horses, rose to the rank of Farrier. He married a Rhodesian woman in 1909, and after discharge from the army worked with horses there until he returned to Bath just before the outbreak of war, where he resumed his trade as a farrier. In August 1914, he joined the Army Service Corps as a Farrier Staff Sergeant and served at Gallipoli with a Veterinary unit in 1915. He came to France in a similar position with a RAMC Field Ambulance of 11th (Northern) Division, and for a reason that remains unknown applied for a commission in 1917. A vacancy was found in the Middlesex Regiment, and he was sent to join the 16th Bn at Ypres. Perhaps considered an unlikely platoon commander, his lifelong army connection with horses continued as he was appointed the unit's transport officer. It was while performing these duties, bringing up the rations for the battalion located in positions north-east of Poelcapelle, that he was killed by a shell.

2/Lt C.Eddy.

FATHER AND SON: The commemoration of brothers is an all too familiar occurrence in the cemeteries and on the memorials of the Western Front battlefields. A woman losing both her husband and son is somewhat rarer, and marks a tragedy impossible to imagine.

103

Lt-Col H.Moorhouse.   **Capt R.Moorhouse.**

Lieutenant Colonel Harry Moorhouse DSO commanded 1/4th Bn King's Own Yorkshire Light Infantry; his son, Ronald Wilkinson Moorhouse MC, was a Captain and company commander in the same unit. On 9th October 1917 the battalion was attacking near the Ravebeek, and Ronald was killed leading his men forward on Belle Vue. His father died only half an hour later, from a stray bullet which struck him as he was leaving his headquarters[1]. The dreadful nature of the ground and terrific shelling meant that after the war their bodies could not be found. One wonders how this double tragedy was compounded for Mrs Moorhouse, having no graves to visit.

Leaving the cemetery, again by the main gate, turn right and follow the minor road as it descends downhill. At the next crossroads turn right, but stop first.

This is the area known as Waterfields and Marsh Bottoms on trench maps. The Canadians took over the front line on Broodseinde Ridge, opposite the village of Passchendaele, from the Australians in late October 1917. Private Donald Fraser, then serving with the Canadian Machine Gun Corps, left a vivid description of the battlefield at this time.

The countryside [was] bare and open and looked as if it had been fought over recently. Shell holes were everywhere and most contained slimy, muddy water. The terrain was a wilderness of mud... We watched the shells send up fountains of mud and water as they exploded. For quite some distance you could see eruptions taking place at various points resembling geysers or mud volcanoes.[2]

The valley is cut by the Ravebeek, a small stream, the banks of which had been smashed by the continuous shellfire from both sides. This flooded the ground and front line conditions for the infantry were almost beyond imagination. In this part of the battlefield British trench maps show no trenches, as such, just a system of inter-connected shell holes forming an outpost line. This meant that all relief had to be done above ground at night, further adding to the problems and misery of battalions going in and out of action here.

Take the right hand road and follow it until another meets it from the left. Stop.

About half way up this road on the right were two position known as Duck Lodge and Snipe Hall. It was here on 30th October 1917, the opening day of the Canadian attack on Passchendaele, that the Princess Patricia's Canadian Light Infantry (PPCLI) moved forward from their assembly positions. As the companies crossed No Man's Land a shell burst and killed one of their officers, Major Talbot Papineau MC. An original PPCLI officer, he was arguably the most important Canadian to die in the Great War – for further details of his life see the entry for the Menin Gate in the Ypres Town Walk. Today he has no known grave, but in 1917 his comrades found his shattered body in a shell hole near Duck Lodge and he was buried on the spot; the grave marked by a rough cross bearing his name. Later, shell fire destroyed it, although the Canadian War Graves office, and his mother, speculated in post-war correspondance[3] that his body may have been found in the 1919 battlefield clearance which took place – perhaps he is in Tyne Cot or Passchendaele New British Cemetery under an unknown soldier's headstone? In the fighting of 30th October Papineau was one of twenty officer casualties in the PPCLI, along with 343 other ranks, of whom 150 were killed. The battalion had numbered twenty-five officers and 600 men that morning, so these losses were heavy. Two members of the unit were awarded Victoria Crosses for their bravery: Lieutenant H.McKenzie was a PPCLI officer attached to the Canadian Machine Gun Corps. He received a posthumous VC for capturing a pillbox, the final attack on which he was killed. Like Talbot Papineau his name is on the Menin Gate. Private G.H.Mullin was the other; am American by birth, he was one of the battalion snipers and survived a similar action against a German pillbox which got him the VC.

Continue as the road climbs the higher ground. Follow it right, then left, until the steps of the Canadian Memorial are reached.

This is Crest Farm. A high point on the battlefield, a small farm complex overlooked the valley where the Canadians attacked in October 1917. The ground here was reached by the 72nd Bn Canadian Infantry (Seaforth Highlanders of Canada) on 30th October, when the unit closely followed their creeping barrage and were able to get into the German positions with minimal losses; 280 all ranks. Canon Scott, a Canadian chaplain, recalled an episode on the battlefield at this time.

The bodies of dead men lay here and there where they had
fallen in the advance. I came across one poor boy who had been

British dead in a German trench at Passchendaele, 1917. (Klaus Späh)

killed that morning. His body was covered with a shiny coating of yellow mud, and looked like a statue made of bronze. He had a beautiful face, with a finely shaped head covered with close curling hair, and looked more like some work of art than a human being.

The huge shell holes were half full of water, often reddened with blood and many of the wounded had rolled down into the pools and been drowned.[4]

After the war Crest Farm was selected as a suitable site for the Canadian Battlefield Memorial commemorating the CEF involvement

'I died in hell...they called it Passchendaele'.

in the battle of Passchendaele. It takes the usual form of a granite block with text in English and Flemish. There is a visitors' book in a bronze locker, which you are invited to sign and leave your comments.

Leave by the steps and turn left, and follow the road around the memorial site. Follow the road past the first turning on the right and continue up to a crossroads where you turn left. This leads to another crossroads. Here turn left and follow the road up to the high ground north of the village. It eventually meets another road; turn left and the cemetery is immediately on the right.

PASSCHENDAELE NEW BRITISH CEMETERY

Passchendaele New British Cemetery in the 1920s: many of the original crosses still remain.

On a ridge overlooking Passchendaele village, the 49th Bn Canadian Infantry attacked this area on 30th October 1917. There was no burial site here during the battle, this being a post-war concentration cemetery. Burials total 1,019 British, 646 Canadian, 292 Australian, 126 New Zealand, four Royal Guernsey Light Infantry, three South African and one Newfoundlander. Of these 1,602 are unknowns – some seventy-five percent.

Outside of Tyne Cot and Lijssenthoek, this is the third largest grouping of Canadian casualties in the Salient. The men buried here, although largely unknown, give a good cross section of the Canadian Expeditionary Force (CEF) at this time. There are immigrant workers from Latvia and Denmark. A Canadian Indian, Private Alexander Decoteau (XI-I-28) was one of many Indians employed as a sniper. He died on 30th October 1917. There are several Americans, often men who had crossed the border in the early part of the war, ashamed their own country was not participating. There are long serving officers like Captain R.Haggard (VII-A-19) of the PPCLI, a 1914 man who had risen from the ranks and commanded a company at Courcelette and Vimy Ridge. He fell not far from Talbot Papineau. Haggard had a literary connection – his uncle was Sir Henry Rider Haggard, author of *King Solomon's Mines*.

A Special Memorial at the rear of the cemetery commemorates the Chaplain of 1/28th Bn London Regiment (Artist's Rifles), Rev. H.Dikinson. He fell on 30th October 1917 when his battalion was attacking alongside the Canadians near a position about a mile from this cemetery, known as Varlet Farm. The Artist's Rifles were an unusual formation, before the war being similar to a gentleman's club, and by late 1914 acting as an officer training unit. It was re-formed in 1917 and became part of the 63rd (Royal Naval) Division, and Passchendaele was its first major action as a front line battalion. The following account of their part in this battle gives a good impression of the problems facing units at this time.

> *Immediately the attack started the forward troops came under intense MG fire from an almost unseen enemy, who were cunningly posted in carefully chosen tactical positions, having taken refuge in the pill-boxes during our intense bombardment... The ground to be traversed was nothing but a deep sea of mud and undoubtedly many men were drowned in the mud-filled shell holes, particularly those who were already wounded. Further, the mud clogged up rifles and Lewis guns in the first few minutes of the attack, and rendered them entirely useless. Consequently it was not long before the attack was brought to a complete standstill.[5]*

The Artist's Rifles had gone into this attack 470 men strong, and had suffered 350 casualties, of whom 170 were killed. Few of these have graves – lost in the mud, their names appear on the Tyne Cot Memorial.

Return via the same route back towards Passchendaele, but at the crossroads go straight on into the main square opposite the church.

Passchendaele, now Passendale, which makes the hissing 's' sound of the name even more sinister, is known more to the locals in this smart Belgian village for its cheese, rather than any connection with the Great War. Many visitors come to Passchendaele and are disappointed; they think of the vast crater zone which covered the battlefield, of the mud and the snow which engulfed the Canadian attacks, and they are not a little saddened to find normality. The only reminder of the fighting in the village itself is a memorial window in the church to the 66th (West Lancs) Division who fought in the approaches for Passchendaele, and a Western Front Association plaque from the 1980s. I once knew a veteran of the battle who in later life showed his son a 1917 aerial photograph of the Passchendaele front, asking him where he thought it was. His son replied, 'the moon', the frightful nature of the ground in this corner of Flanders cannot be overstated. Now we have houses, shops and bars. It is time for the pilgrim to move on.

Leave the main square by the Zonnebeke road (signposted) and follow it for some distance out of the village, keeping to the left. After about twenty minutes walking, a grass path is seen going out across the fields to the left – almost opposite a minor road turning on the right. Take this path to a memorial.

This small memorial commemorates the men of the 85th Bn Canadian Infantry (Nova Scotia Highlanders) who fell in the fighting for Passchendaele. During these operations the battalion suffered heavy casualties, particularly amongst the officers, and the names of the 148 dead are listed here on a bronze plaque. Erected in the spring

In the wasteland of Passchendaele wounded Canadian soldiers and German prisoners await evacuation.

of 1919, a photograph of it appears in the Michelin guide to Ypres published the same year. It is one of only a handful of Canadian battalion memorials on the Western Front.

Return to the main road, go left in the direction of Zonnebeke and continue. A little further along a cycle track is seen going off to the right, on what looks like a sunken road which is tree/scrub lined. It is the route of the old Ypres – Roulers railway line. Follow it for a few hundred yards until it meets a road. Turn right and continue on this road past some houses, and round a corner to Tyne Cot Cemetery and your vehicle.

FOLLOW UP VISIT:

In nearby Zonnebeke is an excellent museum dedicated to the history of the area around Passchendaele. It is located in the old chateau, destroyed in the war and now rebuilt. The chateau grounds are also a suitable place for a picnic with wooden seats, a huge lake and toilets.

Known as the Streekmuseum, and signposted from Tyne Cot, it traces the history of the area from pre-Roman times, but concentrates on the Great War. The fighting is looked at chronologically from 1914 to 1918 using photographs, maps, life-size trench reconstructions with mannequins in original uniforms, and many other interesting artefacts. Many of the photographs are from German sources, and so rarely seen, offering a unique perspective on the operations that took place here. Part of the display also examines the post-war reconstruction of the region, and there are several books and postcards on sale. In 1998 the entrance fee was only 50BF. Recommended.

1 1/4th Bn KOYLI *War Diary,* 9.10.17, PRO WO95/2806.
2 Roy, R.H. *The Journal of Private Fraser* (Sono Nis Press 1985) p.313.
3 This is evident from papers in his personnel file in the Canadian National Archives, which itself runs to over 200 pages; I am grateful to Ron Jack, of MARRS, for his assistance in acquiring a copy of it.
4 Scott, F.G. *The Great War As I Saw It* (Goodchild 1922) p.228.
5 From papers in the archives of Tony & Joan Poucher.

The memorial to the 85th Bn photographed in 1919.

Chapter Seven

BEHIND THE LINES WALK:
BRANDHOEK – VLAMERTINGHE

STARTING POINT: **Brandhoek New Military Cemetery No 3**
DURATION: **4½ hours.**

WALK SUMMARY: *A pleasant walk in the Flemish countryside between Poperinghe and Ypres which was a hive of activity during the Great War. The sites of former camps and casualty clearing stations are also visited, along with associated cemeteries.*

  Park your vehicle outside Brandhoek New Military Cemetery No 3 and take time to visit the cemetery before moving off.

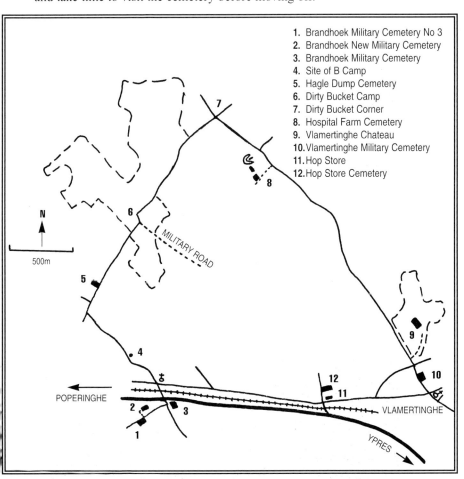

1. Brandhoek Military Cemetery No 3
2. Brandhoek New Military Cemetery
3. Brandhoek Military Cemetery
4. Site of B Camp
5. Hagle Dump Cemetery
6. Dirty Bucket Camp
7. Dirty Bucket Corner
8. Hospital Farm Cemetery
9. Vlamertinghe Chateau
10. Vlamertinghe Military Cemetery
11. Hop Store
12. Hop Store Cemetery

BRANDHOEK NEW MILITARY CEMETERY No 3

One of three cemeteries in the small village of Brandhoek, there were many medical units in and around this area during the fighting for Ypres. New Cemetery No 3 was opened in August 1917 and became the main burial ground for soldiers who died of wounds in the Casualty Clearing Stations (CCS) located at Brandhoek. Used until 1918, a quarter of the graves are men from artillery units who also had their gun sites in the nearby fields. The bronze cemetery gates were given by the family of Lieutenant A.H.Strutt (IV-A-5) of the 16th Bn Sherwood Foresters who died of wounds, received near the Bluff, on 27th April 1918. There are 849 British, forty-six Australian, forty-six Canadian, eighteen New Zealand, five South African, one British West Indies Regiment and one Chinese Labour Corps burials.

Two senior officers were buried here. Lieutenant Colonel T.C.Irving DSO (I-N-26) was a staff officer with 4th (Canadian) Division Engineers and died on 29th October 1917, aged thirty-eight. Lieutenant Colonel S.J.Somerville (II-F-17) was one part of a great family tragedy. He died of wounds, received near the Steenbeek, on 16th August 1917 while serving with 9th Bn Royal Irish Fusiliers. Aged forty-six, and a long serving officer, his son was killed on the Somme in 1916 and buried in Authuille Military Cemetery (see *Walking The Somme*). The register records a further tragic occurrence for an RAMC man. Corporal W.Bathgate (II-B-10), of 113th Field Ambulance, died of wounds 15th August 1917 and 'was laid to rest by his brother Robert (Sergeant 112th Field Amb)'.

Leaving the cemetery turn right, and after only a few yards a CWGC sign on the left indicates a grass path to the next cemetery.

BRANDHOEK NEW MILITARY CEMETERY

This cemetery took over from Brandhoek Military Cemetery in July 1917 when the 3rd (Australian), 32nd and 44th CCSs arrived at Brandhoek in preparation for Third Ypres. It was used in the opening phase of the operations and then closed in August 1917 when the cemetery you have just come from was started. There are 513 British, twenty-eight German, eleven Australian and six Canadian graves in the cemetery.

The most visited grave here is undoubtedly that of Captain Noel Gordon Chavasse VC and bar MC (III-B-15), Royal Army Medical Corps. Chavasse was the medical officer of 1/10th Bn King's Liverpool Regiment (Liverpool Scottish), and served with them from the outbreak of war. He was awarded the MC for bravery at Hooge in

1915 and his first Victoria Cross at Guillemont on the Somme in August 1916. He returned to the Salient with his battalion in time for Third Ypres and was in action at Mouse Trap Farm near Wieltje from 31st July 1917 until he was mortally wounded, dying in a CCS at Brandhoek on 4th August. For further bravery in this attack he was awarded a bar to his VC – one of only three men in the history of the medal to achieve this.

But there are other soldiers at Brandhoek, often overlooked by the casual visitor. In addition to Chavasse a further thirteen RAMC men have graves in the cemetery. Two of them were medical officers like Chavasse: Captain F.R.Armitage DSO (I-E-8), who died of wounds on 30th July 1917, attached to 232nd Bde RFA; and Captain H.D.Willis (VI-F-12), attached to 3rd Bn Worcestershire Regiment, killed on 12th August 1917. Of the others, three in Plot IV, Row D died serving with 47th Sanitary Section on 5th August 1917, a unit rarely encountered but which performed an important job in areas behind the lines where vast numbers of men were camped out.

The other burials are dominated by Irish regiments. Among them is a battalion commander, Lieutenant Colonel T.H.Boardman DSO (III-F-1) who died of wounds 5th August 1917 with 8th Bn Royal Inniskilling Fusiliers. CSM E.Power (III-E-5), a regular of the 2nd Bn Royal Irish Regiment who had served at Mons and was the holder of the Military Cross – rare to Warrant Officers. He died of wounds on 8th August 1917, aged thirty-eight.

Leaving the cemetery return to the road and turn left. Continue to a T-junction and cross another road to the next cemetery, visible opposite.

BRANDHOEK MILITARY CEMETERY

Because of its location and distance from the front, Brandhoek was for much of the war not in range of German field artillery and was therefore considered 'safe'. As such RAMC Field Ambulances operated in the village from 1915 onwards, and as a consequence the cemetery was started by them in May, in a field next to the then Advanced Dressing Station (ADS). The cemetery was closed in July 1917, just prior to Third Ypres. By this time CCSs had replaced the ADS, and they eventually used the two cemeteries you have just come from. Graves here number: 600 British, sixty-three Canadian, four Australian, two Bermuda Rifle Volunteer Corps and two German. Of this number only four are unknown.

The graves are roughly in date order, the earliest ones being close

Brandhoek Military Cemetery in the 1920s.

to the entrance. Artillery units had their gun positions at Brandhoek, and so there are many Royal Artillery graves to be found here. Second Lieutenant Rowland T.Cobbald (I-F-19) was serving in the 6th Battery RFA when he was killed in action on 25th September 1915, aged twenty-three. The register records he returned to England from the Argentine to enlist. Another like him was Second Lieutenant J.S.Leeds (I-D-2), who died on 19th September 1915, aged twenty-eight, while serving with the 1st Honourable Artillery Company. Leeds had returned from Argentina in September 1914. There are several 1st HAC men buried elsewhere in the cemetery, casualties from the almost constant fighting around Hooge. Also among them was a journalist, a writer for the *Daily Chronicle:* Private George Mascord (I-E-5), who died of wounds on 20th September 1915, aged twenty-six.

There are four senior officers in the cemetery, who between them had many years of service. Brigadier General F.J.Heyworth CB DSO (II-C-2) of the Scots Guards died on 9th May 1916, while commanding 3rd Guards Brigade. Lieutenant Colonel C.Conyers (I-C-21) was 'killed while leading a charge of the 2nd Leinsters' at St Eloi on 12th May 1915, aged forty-six. A Boer War veteran, his original unit was the 2nd Bn Royal Irish Fusiliers. Lieutenant Colonel J.Clarke CB (I-B-19) is buried behind him, and died a few days before on 10th May 1915, aged fifty-six. He was serving with the 1/9th Bn Argyll and Sutherland Highlanders when he was mortally wounded during Second Ypres. Also buried close by is Lieutenant Colonel A.F.Sargeaunt (I-D-20) of the Royal Engineers, who died on 31st July 1915, aged forty-four.

Two RFC Balloon officers are buried next to each other; Lieutenant

T.F.Lucas (I-L-1) and Captain E.A.Wickson (I-L-2) were killed when their observation balloon of 20th Balloon Company RFC fell to earth on 16th July 1917. Both men were in their thirties; Wickson had previous service in the 51st Bn Canadian Infantry, and Lucas had a titled father.

Concentrations of graves from one unit are found in Plot II, Row G; a row of men from the 1st Welsh Guards who died of wounds holding the Canal Bank sector near Boesinghe between 1st March and 24th July 1916. Also in Plot II, Row H are twelve graves of men from 42nd Bn Canadian Infantry (Highlanders) who died on 3rd August 1916.

Leaving the cemetery by the gate turn right and walk to the new Poperinghe – Ypres road and cross it via the pedestrian crossing. This is a very busy road and care should be taken. Once across, follow the footpath to the railway and go over that down a minor road.

The railway ran here during the war and by Third Ypres there were several sidings at Brandhoek so the wounded could be brought straight to the CCSs. If they required further treatment, casualties could be taken on other rains along the same line to the main CCS at Remi Siding, south-west of Poperinghe (now Lijssenthoek Cemetery – see Poperinghe Walk), or further to a base hospital on the French coast. On 31st July 1917 and subsequent days, given the number of burials in the Brandhoek cemeteries alone, this must have been a very busy area.

The minor road brings you out into the centre of Brandhoek and onto the old Poperinghe – Ypres road. The church, now rebuilt, is to your right. Go straight across to join Kleine Branderstr. Continue down what soon becomes a quiet country lane.

Further along, past a bend to the right, and just before a white farm cottage, was the site of B Camp. This was one of dozens of military camps between Poperinghe and Ypres which were used during the war years for troops going to and from the line. Many were simply known by a single letter – such as B here – others had more unusual names like Chippewaw and MicMac. Conditions in these camps varied greatly; some had tents, others wooden huts or even the newly designed Nissen Huts. An officer of the 12th Bn Rifle Brigade recalled a typical camp like B Camp at the time of Third Ypres in 1917.

There are about twenty bivouacs per company and every officers' mess has a big tarpaulin as head-cover. With numerous 4.5 ammunition boxes and sundry pieces of timber... which we found in close proximity to our camp, the place was soon made quite comfortable.[1]

Canadian troops fraternise with Belgian girls behind the lines near Poperinghe, 1917.

Continue along this route, past several old Flemish houses, until it meets another road. Turn right at this junction and a little further up on the left is Hagle Dump Cemetery.

HAGLE DUMP CEMETERY

Hagle Dump was the name given to a large ammunition and supply depot two miles south-west of Elverdinghe and close to the site of this cemetery. Nearby was another camp, used extensively during the

fighting of 1917-18, but the cemetery itself was not started until April 1918 during the Battle of Lys. It remained in use until October, and after the war 207 graves were moved in from various points in the Ypres Salient to what is now Plots III and IV. Twenty-six Americans and two French soldiers were moved to other cemeteries. Today there are 397 British, twenty-six Australian, fourteen Canadian and two German burials. Of this number 142 are unknown.

Many of the original graves in Plot I represent behind the lines units that operated in this area: Siege Battery gunners, Light Railway units and Army Tramway companies. However, in Plot I, Rows C and D, is a large concentration of men from the 10th Bn Royal West Kents, all of whom died on 27th April 1918. They bear testimony to the folly of placing a rest camp so close to an ammunition dump. Their *War Diary* records what happened that day.

> *A serious explosion occurred behind the Detail Camp about 12.30pm caused by a H.V. [High Velocity] enemy shell striking an ammunition and gun cotton dump. The camp was wrecked and numerous huts set on fire by the explosion. Rescue parties at once set to work to assist in recovering the numerous casualties from the debris, and extinguishing the fires, in face of great danger from recurring explosions.*[2]

Lieutenant D.F.Anderson (I-D-7) was among the dead, along with seventeen other ranks. A further twenty-eight men were wounded and one man missing. The blow to the battalion was heavy; most of the dead and wounded were Warrant Officers and Sergeants, arguably the men who keep a unit together in the field – indeed there are two CQMS and four Sergeants buried in this plot.

Elsewhere in the cemetery there are some interesting inscriptions on headstones. On that of private F.C.Healy (III-E-11), 1/4th Suffolks, who died on 25th September 1917, it is simply stated, 'A Gamekeeper'. Second Lieutenant A.C.Ransdale (II-G-6) '...came from the Argentine at his nation's call for help'. He was killed with the 15th Bn Loyal North Lancs on 1st September 1918. An unusually named soldier was Private William Henry Jubilee Kitchen (III-F-15) who died with 1st Bn Gloucestershire Regiment on 1st November 1914, aged twenty-seven. One must presume he was born on or close to one of Queen Victoria's jubilees?

Leaving the cemetery turn left and continue along the road. There is a useful shop close to the cemetery, which sells drinks, food and other supplies and is usually open. Soon the road approaches a large wooded area and enters it from the south side. On a sharp bend, with a house set in the wood to your left, a noticeboard just to the left of the road records the fact that these woods once contained Dirty Bucket Camp.

A typical British camp behind the lines.

Officers of the London Regiment practise gas mask drill at Dirty Bucket Camp, August 1917.

Dirty Bucket Camp was one of the largest camps in the Salient during the Great War, and in fact was a series of hutted and tented areas covering several square miles. Some were in the wood itself, others bordered on it. It took its name from a local estaminet known to the troops as The Dirty Bucket, and the modern noticeboard on this bend gives further information in English and Flemish about the camp. An officer of the 11th Bn Royal Fusiliers felt that Dirty Bucket Camp was '... a very aptly named place.'[3] Edwin Campion Vaughan was serving as an officer in the Royal Warwickshire Regiment and came to the area in August 1917.

> *... we turned off to the left towards Dirty Bucket Corner and shortly halted outside a wood wherein our camp lay. It was a nondescript camp consisting of bivouacs, tents, huts and tarpaulin shelters into which we stowed the troops as best we could. For our combined mess and bedroom we had a small hut with a table and a couple of forms. It was a baleful place for the shell holes and shattered trees bore testimony to the attentions of the German gunners. Amongst the trees was a great concentration of tanks – and the name of the camp was Slaughter Wood![4]*

From this bend a plank road took troops from the camp along what was known as Military Road all the way to Vlamtinghe, and from there up to the front line around Ypres. Although the planks have long gone, a track can be seen going through the trees but it is a private road now and cannot be entered. Edmund Blunden recalled this route just prior to Third Ypres when he was here with the 11th Bn Royal Sussex Regiment (1st South Downs).

> *Wooden tracks led this way and that in puzzling number through the crowded airless shadows, and new roads threw open... a district only suited for the movements of a small and careful party. At the corner where one swaggering highway left the wood eastward, an enormous model of the German systems... was open for inspection, whether from the ground or from stepped ladders raised beside, and this was popular, though whether from its charm as a model or value as a military aid is uncertain.*[5]

Tens of thousands of British soldiers spent their time out of the trenches at this camp. It was often shelled. Prior to Third Ypres long range German runs fired at Dirty Bucket, and German Gotha bombers were also active in the area from 1917. In one such incident men of C Bn Tank Corps came under fire on 4th July 1917 when the battalion orderly room was hit wounding two officers and two men, killing four Gunners and a Corporal. A tank also received a direct hit, damaging a sponson, breaking some rollers and cutting the track[6]. No doubt amongst the trees are vestiges of the old camp, but sadly this ground is also private land and cannot be entered.

Continue along the road, and as you come out of the main wood there are good views to your right. On clear days Vlamtinghe can be seen, and the distant farm in the fields is Hospital Farm – the Cross of Sacrifice from the cemetery there also visible. During the war the vast sprawl of camps from Dirty Bucket continued into these fields.

Indian troops prepare their food near Vlamtinghe, 1914.

Follow the road to a crossroads – Dirty Bucket Corner – here turn right and continue until you are parallel with a farm – Hospital Farm – in the fields to your right, A little further on a green CWGC sign can be seen. Go through the turnstile gate, and follow a line of trees to the cemetery entrance.

HOSPITAL FARM CEMETERY

This rarely visited cemetery is in an unspoilt, quiet and secluded spot, typical of the area between Poperinghe and Ypres. Hospital Farm was the name given to several farm buildings, which you have passed on the way into the cemetery. These were used by the RAMC as an ADS, cases being evacuated back here from Elverdinghe and Vlamertinghe station. During the war a light tramway ran close to the farm. The ADS was expanded by the West Riding Field Ambulances of the 49th (West Riding) Division when they held the Canal Bank sector at Boesinghe in mid to late 1915. Graves total 116 – all but one is British, the other a French civilian killed nearby in August 1916.

Aside from the ADS, there were many gun sites in the Hospital Farm area, and the graves here reflect this. Three officers from 21st (1st Lancs) Heavy Battery RGA are buried side by side: Captain A.D.MacNeil (B-5), Captain R.W.C.M.Rodgers (B-6) and Lieutenant A.E.Voysey (B-4). All died on 27th July 1917, in the lead up to Third Ypres when the number of artillery units operating on this part of the front were expanded greatly; there were 752 heavy howitzers and 1,422 field guns participating in the preliminary bombardment by this time.

Lieutenant Lambert Playfair (B-9) was an early officer of the Royal Flying Corps. Born in India, his parents lived in Upper Assam, and educated at Sandhurst (where he won a prize cadetship), Playfair was commissioned into the 1st Bn Royal Scots in January 1913, later joining the RFC as an observer. On 6th July 1915, while serving with No 1 Squadron, his Avro 504 was on artillery observation duties over St Julien. At 11.04am his pilot came into combat with two German Aviatiks, a burst of machine-gun fire hit the Avro's engine, and Playfair was found to be dead when the aircraft made a forced landed near Hospital Farm.

Lieutenant Lambert Playfair

The cemetery register indicates further evidence of the German bombing raids on the camps around Hospital Farm and Dirty Bucket Corner. RSM W.Walker (E-24), of the 1/4th Bn Gordon Highlanders, is recorded as having been 'killed by a bomb from a German aeroplane' on 15th September 1917. A soldier of the same unit, killed the same day, is buried next to him.

Return to the road via the same route you accessed the cemetery, and turn right after the turnstile. From here it is about thirty minutes walk into Vlamertinghe along a quiet and pleasant route.

Just as you approach the outskirts of the village, a small park borders the road on the left, and soon some large white gates are visible. This is a private drive, but respecting this go in and look at Vlamertinghe chateau – an impressive building. Poet Edmund Blunden was here with 11th Bn Royal Sussex Regiment in July 1917 and recalled the visit in the following poem.

Vlamertinghe: Passing The Chateau July 1917

'And all her silken flanks with garlands dressed' –
But we are coming to the sacrifice.
Must those have flowers who are not yet gone West?
May those have flowers who live with death and lice?
This must be the floweriest place
That earth allows; the queenly face
Of the proud mansion borrows grave for grace
Spite of those brute guns lowing at the skies.
Bold great daisies' golden lights,
Bubbling roses' pinks and whites –
Such a gay carpet! Poppies by the million;
Such damask! Such vermilion!
But if you ask me, mate, the choice of colour
Is scarcely right; this red should have been duller.[7]

A plaque by the chateau records this poem in Flemish.

Continue into Vlamertinghe and the military cemetery is on the left.

VLAMERTINGHE

VLAMERTINGHE MILITARY CEMETERY

Started by French troops in 1914, six British burials were made here at that time and are now in the north-west corner. Field Ambulances operating in Vlamertinghe then used the cemetery, as did fighting units returning from the line to bury their dead. It was closed in June 1917, as there was no further space available, the ground surrounding the cemetery then being used by railway units. Burials thereafter moved to Vlamertinghe New Military Cemetery south of the village. In total there are 1,114 graves of British soldiers, fifty-two Canadians, four Australians, two South Africans, two Newfoundlanders, one Indian and one German. The wrought iron gates were given by Lord Redesdale in memory of his son, Major the Hon. C.B.O.Mitford DSO (I-E-8) who was killed on Frezenberg Ridge with the 10th Hussars on 13th May 1915, aged thirty-eight, and is buried here.

Of the total number of graves, nearly 250 are soldiers from Lancashire Territorial units, largely men in 55th (West Lancs) Division who in early 1917 buried their dead in this cemetery; both soldiers who died of wounds and those killed in the front line – now in Plots IV, V and VI. There are also a large number of officers and men from Cavalry units who fell in the fighting on Frezenberg Ridge in May 1915, such as Major Mitford above. Among them are other officers from equally well known families: Captain Guy Bonham-Carter (I-G-3), 19th Hussars, killed 15th May 1915, and Captain Francis Octavius Grenfell VC (II-B-14), 9th Lancers, died 24th May 1915. Twin brother of Riversdale, and cousin of poet Julian, Francis had been awarded the Victoria Cross for saving the guns at Audregnies on 24th August 1914. The Grenfells lost heavily in the war; brother Riversdale fell on the Aisne, and the fighting at Frezenberg eventually consumed Julian, and Francis himself. Elsewhere are two other important Frezenberg casualties: Lieutenant Colonel E.R.A.Shearman (I-D-7) and Captain & Adjutant G.C.Stewart (I-D-6), both of whom died on 13th May 1915 serving with the 10th Hussars.

Other interesting graves include Corporal C.E.Brookes (VII-B-9), 8th Bn Royal West Kents, killed in action on 27th May 1917, who, the register records, 'after serving over 18 months on the battlefields he was killed on the eve of obtaining his commission'. Private N.Finucane (V-C-11) was 'one of the crew of the Lusitania', surviving its sinking, served at Gallipoli, but was killed with the 1/10th Bn King's Liverpool Regiment near Ypres on 4th January 1917.

Second Lieutenant Harold Parry (VI-L-12) is shown in the register as 'one of England's soldier poets'. Born in 1896, he was educated at Queen Mary's Grammar School and won a scholarship to Oxford in 1915. After only a short period as a student he decided to enlist and was commissioned in 1916. He later joined the 17th Bn King's Royal Rifle Corps. Serving with them on the Somme, from his experiences there he wrote the following poem which was humorously entitled 'River that runs into everyone's dugout'.

I come from trenches deep in slime,
Soft slime so sweet and yellow,
And rumble down the steps in time
To souse 'some shivering fellow'.

I trickle in and trickle out
Of every nook and corner,
And, rushing like some waterspout,
Make many a rat a mourner.

I gather in from near and far
A thousand brooklets swelling,
And laugh aloud a great 'Ha ha!'
To flood poor Tommy's dwelling.[8]

British transport pass their French comrades on the road into Vlamtinghe, 1914.

Parry came to Ypres with his battalion in November 1916, and was killed somewhere on the Yser canal sector by shellfire on 6th May 1917. His poems were published posthumously in 1918, in a memoir prepared by his family.

Leave by the cemetery gate and turn left, going into the centre of Vlamertinghe. Continue to the church.

Vlamertinghe was a main route up to Ypres and the front line trenches, and during the major offensives – particularly Third Ypres – the roads here were crowded with traffic, guns and limbers, ambulances, lorries and buses. Virtually every division going up to the fighting north-east of Ypres came through this village. The chateau was used as a headquarters, buildings in the village became store dumps and depots, billets for the troops and quarters for the many artillery units in operation here. RAMC Field Ambulances established several ADS, the most famous of which was in Vlamertinghe Mill; of which there is sadly no trace today. There are several bars and shops in the village, and a visit to the church is worthwhile if you have the time.

From the church go west on the road to Poperinghe. Follow this for some distance, passing on the left the site of Vlamertinghe windmill. Henry Williamson described the scene here during the Battle of the Menin Road Ridge in September 1917.

There was a Casualty Clearing Station in the boarded mill beside the road... Inside the lower rooms white sheets hung on the walls, and across the ceilings. Two RAMC surgeons, in white aprons, smoked unconcernedly outside. They had been at work on case after case all day. A convoy of motor ambulances was arriving. Lightly wounded men, more or less content, having had their wounds dressed, were sitting in the shade of elms lining the road, smoking and talking as they awaited transport to the train. Their faces were almost carved in earth by dried sweat-runs through grime.[9]

Continue until the outskirts of the village are reached. Almost the last building on the right is a large brick-built Hop Store which was also used as an ADS during the Great War. It bears the date 1868 and is virtually in its original condition. Just past the Hop Store is a CWGC sign indicating a minor road which takes you to the cemetery of the same name.

HOP STORE CEMETERY

Medical units established an ADS in the Hop Store in early 1915, and burials began in May of that year. The cemetery expanded, and many more graves were added in 1917 during Third Ypres. One Canadian and 247 British soldiers are buried in the cemetery. Fifty-eight of them are men from artillery units, reflecting the many gun sites in this area, and there are also a number of RAMC personnel.

An unusual headstone is that of Major H.P.Philby DSO (I-A-16). Philby was a regular army officer, having been commissioned into the York and Lancaster Regiment in September 1908. His service before the Great War included an attachment to the West African Frontier Force, and he returned to England in August 1914 to join the 2nd York and Lancs, then on its way to France. He fought on the Aisne, at First Ypres, and was awarded the Distinguished Service Order for bravery at Hooge on 9th August 1915. By the end of that year he was acting adjutant, and moved to the Canal Bank sector, where he was appointed to command the battalion in early 1916; although he did not live long enough to be promoted to the rank of Lieutenant Colonel. Philby met his death opposite Morteldje estaminet, north-east of Ypres, on the night of 17th/18th May 1916. A much beloved officer, his body was brought back to Vlamertinghe by his men. One wonders what such a long serving and brave officer would have made of his nephew, the spy Kim Philby?

The graves are roughly in date order and the lettering on many of them is of a different style encountered in other cemeteries. This was one of the earliest cemeteries constructed at Ypres by the IWGC, who were then still experimenting with style and design. In Plot I, Rows D and E are the graves of men from

Major H.P.Philby, 2nd York & Lancs.

a variety of famous cavalry regiments, all of whom died during Second Ypres in 1915. Among them are two officers of the 1st Dragoons who died of wounds received at Frezenberg Ridge in May: Captain W.H.J. St Leger Atkinson (I-D-18), aged thirty-three, and Captain H.McLaren Lambert (I-D-17), aged thirty-six.

Returning to the Poperinghe road turn right in the direction of Poperinghe itself. It is wise to cross the road to the southern side, as there is a cycle lane and occasionally this route can be busy: however beware of cyclists; especially at the weekend!

Many troops marched down this road during the Great War and its then cobbled surface would have echoed to the sound of thousands of British army boots. In this direction, knowing that a billet in one of the many camps lay ahead of them, such men might have been singing: a good commanding officer allowed the men to talk in the ranks if the route ahead was not too long. Files of soldiers coming in the opposite direction, heading for Ypres and the front line, would have looked on with envy. These silent columns passed their happy comrades with unmoving faces – particularly if they knew what lay ahead.

Stay on this road until it brings you back into Brandhoek. In the village it is wiser to use the pavement, rather than remain on the road. Past the modern church, take a turning on the left down a road used earlier in the walk; Branderstr. Cross the railway and busy main road, and then turn right following the CWGC sign back to the Brandhoek cemeteries and your vehicle.

1 Seymour, W.W. *The History of the Rifle Brigade in the War of 1914-1918* Vol II (Rifle Brigade Club Ltd 1936) p.120.
2 10th Bn Royal West Kent Regiment *War Diary*, PRO WO95/2638.
3 O'Neill, H.C. *The Royal Fusiliers in the Great War* (Heinemann 1922) p.199.
4 Vaughan, E.C. *Some Desperate Glory* (Frederick Warne Ltd 1981) p.190.
5 Blunden, E. *Undertones of War* (Cobdean Sanderson 1928) p.192-3.
6 C Bn Tank Corps *War Diary*, 4.7.17, PRO WO95/106. The fatalities were once buried in Oosthoek Wood, part of Dirty Bucket Camp, but their graves were moved to Gwalia Cemetery, near Poperinghe, after the war.
7 Blunden op cit. p.256.
8 Parry, H. *In Memoriam* (WH Smith 1918).
9 Williamson, H. *Love And The Loveless* (Panther Books 1963) p.253.

Chapter Eight

POPERINGHE TOWN WALK

STARTING POINT: **Railway Station, Poperinghe.**
DURATION: **2 hours (depending on the time spent in Talbot House).**

WALK SUMMARY: *This short walk visits the main sites in central Poperinghe, including the famous 'Talbot House' where Toc-H began in 1915. It also recommends two follow-up visits to nearby military cemeteries, which are too far to include in the scope of this walk.*

You can either leave your vehicle in the parking area outside the railway station (remember to buy a ticket!), or you could leave it in Ypres itself and sample Belgian railways by taking the train to Poperinghe; times are available from the tourist office or at the railway station in Ypres. Return fares are inexpensive, and there are reasonably frequent trains.

Poperinghe, alternatively known as Pop or Pops to the British Tommy, was an important bastion in the lines of communication behind the Ypres Salient during the Great War. A town of 12,000 inhabitants in 1914, it was never completely evacuated and as such was

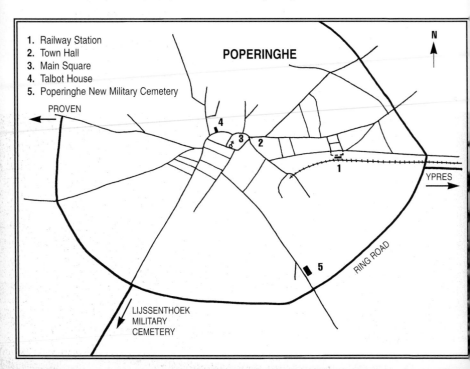

1. Railway Station
2. Town Hall
3. Main Square
4. Talbot House
5. Poperinghe New Military Cemetery

POPERINGHE

N

PROVEN

YPRES

RING ROAD

LIJSSENTHOEK MILITARY CEMETERY

often seen as something of an oasis by British troops out of the trenches. Many houses, factories and other buildings were commandeered for use as headquarters, administrative offices, billets, baths and even semi-legalised brothels. In the fields and hamlets around the town vast hutted camps were constructed and large medical establishments erected, around which grew military cemeteries. Military detention camps run by the Military Provost Staff Corps were also located at Poperinghe (including in the town hall – see below), where deserters and defaulters were kept awaiting trial, or as part of their punishment. Some suffered the ultimate fate and were 'shot at dawn'; executed for a number of different military crimes.

Troops were always in Poperinghe, and the local inhabitants came to know men from every corner of the British Empire. Because the civilians remained in the town, soldiers were able to visit and enjoy the famous 'estaminets' – where food and drink could be obtained, and one of the few places where men could actually relax and forget the war. Local photographers did a roaring trade in portrait photographs, and shops sold picture postcards, silks and other souvenirs to send home to family and friends. Officers had their own restaurants and cafés, but all mixed together in Talbot House, just off the main square, where there were films and shows to entertain them. Although it suffered from shellfire and bombing, particularly in 1918, Poperinghe was never damaged to the extent Ypres was and retains many of its original buildings today. It is an attractive and quiet Flemish town, with many good restaurants and hotels, and offers a suitable alternative to Ypres as a base for touring the area.

Poperinghe station was an important railway junction for the British forces in the Salient. Linked to the railhead of Hazebrouck, in France, troop and supply trains could move up here from any of the channel

Indian troops in Rue d'Ypres, Poperinghe, 1915.

ports and the major camps behind the lines at Etaples or Rouen. Men of the Royal Engineers Railway Operating Department (ROD) took over the organisation of Poperinghe station almost as soon as the BEF arrived here in 1914, and continued to do so for the rest of the war. Some distance from the battlefield, Poperinghe was rarely threatened by concentrated shellfire – perhaps the occasional long-range shell – but by 1917 the Germans were operating Gotha bombing raids over the town and the railway became a prime target. A main route to and from the Salient, officers and men went on, and returned from, leave at this station, tens of thousands of troops arrived here in cattle trucks marked 'Hommes 40, Chevaux 8' – and how many of them on a one way journey to a shallow grave in Flanders? Henry Williamson remembered a visit in 1917. By this time trains could not stop at the main platforms as they had been so badly damaged. A new siding was therefore made further up the track.

> The troops trains arriving at 'Pop' by day used to behave peculiarly as they approached the station through acres of hospital hutments and military cemeteries. Card parties squatting on the floors of the wooden trucks were liable to be thrown forwards, jerked upright, and flung backwards. Cling! – clang! – plonk! – plink! – crank! ran from buffer to buffer along the grey length of the train. Then another jerk, the frantic puffing of an engine whose wheels were racing on the rails, and the train went on, faster and faster, rattling through the station, and stopping half a mile past it.[1]

British and French troops mix with local civilians on Poperinghe station, 1914.

Four Gunners from the RFA, together with their mascot 'Kemmel', photographed in Poperinghe 1915.

Harry Kendall, serving with the King Edward's Horse in the Poperinghe area about this time recalled that many of the troops noticed how regularly the shells arrived just as a train was approaching, and many suspected the civilian stationmaster, who Kendall claimed was later shot as a traitor.

Leaving the station by the main entrance cross the square in front onto a road that runs left to right, Ieperstraat.

This was known as Rue d'Ypres in 1914 and there were cafés and restaurants here during the war, and many local photographers offering cheap portraits and group photographs. A few shops existed, but low pay in the British army meant that the average Tommy could rarely afford any luxuries. Some of these houses in this street were used as billets in the early part of the war, and the occupants were not always accommodating to their allies. Lieutenant Colonel John Humphrey, the Town Major of Poperinghe, recorded in July 1915,

> ...*Monsieur Emile, Rue d'Ypres, complains of damage done to his property by British soldiers billeted there – statue broken 75F, crockery 25F; forwarded a claim to APM V Corps.*[2]

He also records that prostitutes were active at No 51 in the same street, one being forcibly evacuated on 20th July 1915 because of Venereal Disease. In September a house at No 94 was broken into and 170 bottles of alcohol stolen; the culprits, whether civilian or military, were never discovered!

In Ieperstraat turn left towards the centre of Poperinghe, but take the first road on the right, Proctstraat. This is only a short road. At the end turn left onto Bruggestraat and follow for some distance past a small square set back from the road, on the left. After this the street becomes G.Gezellestraat. A little way further on, the town hall building is on the left. Follow the entrance into the main courtyard.

The Town Hall is in the centre of Poperinghe and it was here that a number of soldiers sentenced to death, following a Field General Courts Martial (FGCM), were executed. The courtyard was arranged with a sandbagged wall at one end and a wooden execution post placed in front. A firing party then carried out the sentence, usually at dawn, with an officer on hand to implement the 'coup de grace' if death was not instantaneous, a chaplain, and a medical officer to pronounce life was extinct and issue a death certificate. Considering this courtyard is only a short distance from the main square, troops in, and coming to and from, Poperinghe would have certainly heard what was going on. But perhaps this was all part of the 'for the sake of example' process these executions were meant to perform. Wilfred Saint-Mande in his fictionalised memoirs, *War, Wine and Women,* recalled a FGCM and execution near here in 1916.

> *One night a private lost his nerve as we were going up to the trenches with ammunition, rations and stores. The shelling was too much for him, and he disappeared into the darkness... nothing was heard of him for fourteen days; he was then arrested at le Havre wearing civilian clothes. The military policemen who caught him said he was hanging about at the docks, trying to sneak on a ship bound for England.*
>
> *The scene in court was impressive, and I had a foreboding that he was doomed... He had enlisted in the first days of the war at the age of eighteen and had been in many fierce engagements. However, according to military law the crime was clear and so was the penalty...The prisoner was sentenced to death and the sentence was carried out at dawn a few days later. We formed up in a large square and the prisoner had to be dragged to a post in the middle of the ground. He was gagged and bound before being*

blindfolded. The firing party looked stern and grim.... After the wretch had been tied to the post his hands kept twitching and his limbs trembled...An officer dropped a handkerchief and the volley rang out.[3]

The first execution took place at Poperinghe in 1916, and the last in 1919 when a soldier of the Chinese Labour Corps was shot for murder. In the courtyard, now encased in plastic, is one of the original execution posts standing roughly where it would have done during the war. Bullet holes and blood stains are grimly visible, and it dates from that last execution in 1919.[4]

Going back towards the road, on the left is the entrance to the so-called 'death cells' (open daily 9am – 5.30pm). These were ancient cells attached to the town hall and used by the local police. The British army took them over during the Great War, and they became a holding pen for soldiers arrested in Poperinghe before being moved on for trial, back to their battalion or on to a proper military prison. It is also believed that several men executed in the courtyard were also detained here the night before their deaths. The cells are now restored and on the walls is a great deal of original graffiti from men held prisoner here. In the right hand cell there is some very crude American 'artwork' from when the 27th and 30th (US) Divisions were here in 1918. The local town council are to be congratulated for preserving this important part of Poperinghe's history.

Leave the cells and return to G.Gezellestraat. Turn left and follow the wall of the town hall into the main square. To your left, in the basement of the town hall itself, is the local tourist office (Tel: 057.33.40.81.) As at Ypres all the staff speak very good English and are happy to provide information about the town or any answer any queries. You can also pick up a very good free leaflet, entitled *'Poperinghe in the First World War'*; English editions are available. Piet Chielen's excellent *Pop.Route* is on sale here (see Bibliography).

Going back into the square, cross it to the other side. There are several bars and restaurants, if needed. Then take a road to the left of a large bar called De La Paix and go into Gasthuisstraat. Follow it for several hundred yards to a building on the right, signposted Talbot House.

Perhaps the most famous building in the Salient, Talbot House was a Belgian town house acquired in 1915, by two 6th Division chaplains, Rev. Neville Talbot and Rev. P.B. 'Tubby' Clayton. They set to work

133

The main square in Poperinghe, 1914.

French cavalry pass through the main square during First Ypres.

with men from the 16th Bn London Regiment (Queen's Westminster Rifles) creating an oasis out of the front line for men billeted in or passing through Poperinghe. Named after Clayton's friend, and Neville's brother, – Gilbert Talbot of the Rifle Brigade who fell at Hooge in 1915 – the house opened soon after his death. An early sign placed by the entrance warned visitors to 'abandon rank all ye who enter' and both officers and men mixed freely inside. There was a library, a cinema in the cellar showing Charlie Chaplain films, a concert hall, quiet rooms for relaxation and letter writing, and even rooms available for those given leave but having nowhere to go or not wanting to return to England. Notice boards, where soldiers could leave details of their name and unit, helped friends and brothers stay in touch. In the hop loft was a chapel, the altar made from an old carpenter's bench, where over 20,000 soldiers attended services between 1915 and 1918. The genesis of the Toc-H organisation started here, and throughout the war Tubby Clayton stayed with his beloved house. However, in 1919 the owner returned and it went back to being a residential dwelling. Toc-H recovered the building again ten years later when Lord Wakenfield bought it on their behalf. It has remained open ever since, and during the Second World War many of its treasures were hidden by the local population.

Today visitors find a hearty welcome from Jacques Ryckebosch and his staff. To gain entrance ring the bell by the main door and someone will come and greet you. Often there are English members of Toc-H on duty and, if available, Jacques will be pleased to give you a tour of the house. Funding has allowed Toc-H to install an excellent slide presentation about the history of the house, and most recently the old concert hall, where thousands of soldiers enjoyed shows during the war, has been purchased. Research by Jacques indicates that the famous comedy duo, Flanagan and Allen, met at Talbot House in 1917, and performed in the concert hall – probably their first ever performance together. It is easy to spend many happy and rewarding hours here, but whatever, no visit is complete without a long climb to the hop loft chapel ('The Upper Room'), preserved as it was during the war. The original carpenter's bench is still there, and a roll of honour records men confirmed in the chapel and later fell in action. The original cross from Gilbert Talbot's grave is on the wall, and one from an unknown soldier's grave hangs above the altar. The atmosphere in this place of tranquillity is like no other, and we must all be grateful to Toc-H for allowing continued access to it. No entrance fee is charged at Talbot House, but donations are welcome and there are a range of postcards and books on sale, including many of the *Battleground Europe* series. Rooms are still available for those visiting the Salient, on a self-catering basis, and are among the cheapest 'billets' in Flanders. But Talbot House is always very busy and early booking is advised (Tel: 057.33.32.28.)

Leaving the house return to Gasthuisstraat and turn right. Further up, on the right, is a building with a sign above it; 'Skindles'.

Skindles was a famous restaurant and club frequented by officers during the Great War. This is not the original – it was located in Rue du Nord (now Casselstraat) – but one that opened in the 1920s and was

The Upper Room at Talbot House.

A typical British concert party.

used by pilgrims to the battlefields between the wars. It closed many years ago and is now a private house, and should be respected as such. Skindles was originally the Hotel de la Bourse du Houblon. It got its wartime name from an officer of the Rifle brigade who, in June 1916, remarked to a friend over a plate of egg and chips, accompanied by a bottle of wine, that it was as good as a pub called Skindles in Maidenhead. The name stuck and the three rooms on the ground floor were always full.

Continue along this street and follow as it bends left, then take the first road on the left, Priesterstraat. Follow to the end and continue on the road that circles the church on your left. Just before the town hall is a road to the right, Ieperstraat – and signposted for Ieper. Take this and follow it back to the railway station. The walk takes about twenty minutes.

FOLLOW UP VISITS: -

There are a number of interesting military cemeteries in and around Poperinghe, but two are particularly important and should be visited as a follow-up to this walk.

POPERINGHE NEW MILITARY CEMETERY

This cemetery is in Poperinghe itself and located just off the main ring road in Deken De Bolaan opposite the road to Reninghelst. It is well signposted. There is parking in a lay-by outside the cemetery, or by a shop opposite.

While Poperinghe grew as a British military base, soldiers who died in the medical establishments, or were brought back from the line, were buried in the communal cemetery on the Reninghelst road. This became known as the Old Cemetery and was started during First Ypres in 1914. Graves were added until May 1915 when a New Military Cemetery was opened on this site in June and remained in use until the end of the war. There were no post-war concentrations of graves into the cemetery, and the total burials number: 596 British, fifty-five Canadian, twenty Australian, three New Zealand, two British West Indies, one Chinese Labour Corps and three unknowns. A separate plot of French and Belgian soldiers is adjacent to the cemetery.

Poperinghe, 1914.

Today Poperinghe New Military Cemetery is frequently visited because of its connections with the executions that took place in and around the town during the Great War. Buried here are seventeen soldiers executed for various military crimes which fell under the main categories of cowardice and desertion. Their stories are well related in *Shot At Dawn,* and readers are directed to that publication for further information.

Visitors should remember that there are others buried in the cemetery, also worthy of consideration. Senior officers are numerous. Lieutenant Colonel G.H.Baker (II-G-1) died of wounds on 2nd June 1916, aged thirty-eight. Commanding 5th Canadian Mounted Rifles, he was mortally wounded during the German attacks on Hill 62. The son of a member of the Senate of Canada, he himself was a member of the Canadian House of Commons. Lieutenant Colonel R.V.Doherty-Howell DSO (II-B-12) was a senior Sapper; Assistant Director of Army Signals of VIII Corps, he was killed near Ypres on 9th January 1917. A titled senior officer was Lieutenant Colonel Sir R.B.N.Gunter (II-H-21) of the Yorkshire Regiment, a regular army soldier who died of wounds on 16th August 1917, aged forty-six. Lieutenant Colonel H.S.Smith DSO (I-E-23) was another regular, aged forty-seven, who was killed commanding 1st Bn Leicestershire Regiment on 22nd October 1915. In addition there are eleven officers with the rank of Major in this cemetery. Captain H.H.Maclean MC (II-G-35), a Highland Light Infantry officer serving as Brigade Major to 153rd Brigade, was 'killed in action by shell fire with his own GOC' on 29th July 1917. His GOC was Brigadier General A.F.Gordon CMG DSO, who is buried in Lijssenthoek cemetery – see below.

Family tragedies are also evident. Private G.Ryan (II-C-8) died of wounds received in a gas attack on the 2nd Hampshires at Potijze on 9th August 1916. The register records, 'his brother, Pte H.Ryan, was also killed on the same day'. Among the many RE tunnellers in the cemetery is Lieutenant E.J.Maxwell-Stuart (I-B-29). From Arundel, Sussex, he was killed with 175th Tunnelling Company on 26th April 1916, being 'one of four brothers killed in the war'.

LIJSSENTHOEK MILITARY CEMETERY

To reach this cemetery take the Poperinghe ring road and make a left hand turn south-west of the town following the sign for Abeele, or Abele. This road eventually crosses the border into France. Follow it before that for a few kilometres, and take a minor road to the left following a green CWGC signpost for the cemetery. At a crossroads, with a café on your left, turn right and continue along this road to the main entrance of the cemetery.

The main road you used to get here was at one time a railway line which ran from Hazebrouck, in France, to Poperinghe. During the war it was a main arterial route for British soldiers coming to and from the Salient, and branch lines were tapped off to camps and depots. One ran to a small farm complex, still visible to the rear of the cemetery, which the British called Remi Farm, or Remi Sidings. RAMC Casualty Clearing Stations were established at Remi in June 1915, and remained in use until the spring of 1918 when long range shell fire forced them further back. Field Ambulances then took over, from both the British and French forces operating in Flanders at that time. Twenty-four soldiers, now in Plot XXXI, were brought in from isolated locations near Poperinghe after the war. These were the only concentrations. Burials total:

British	7,350	South African	29
Australian	1,131	Unknown	22
Canadian	1,053	British West Indies	21
French	658	Newfoundland	5
New Zealand	291	American	3
German	223	Indian	2
Chinese Labour Corps	32	War Graves Commission	1

Lijssenthoek Cemetery in 1919,

Next to Tyne Cot this is the largest British military cemetery in the Salient, but gives the visual impression of being much bigger. It is arguably a much more important cemetery than Tyne Cot, as all but twenty-two of the men buried here are known; at Tyne Cot most are unknowns. Lijssenthoek therefore represents a good cross-section of not only the type of men who served in the Ypres Salient, but also the types of units and men that made up the army as a whole.

Given the variation and scope of the units in this cemetery, it is quite possible that every rank in the army up to major general is represented on a headstone. Indeed, senior officers are particularly noticeable with one major general, three brigadier generals and sixteen lieutenant colonels. Major General M.S.Mercer CB (VI-A-38) was the most senior Canadian officer to die at Ypres; he was mortally wounded commanding 3rd (Canadian) Division at Hill 62 on 3rd June 1916. Brigadier General A.F.Gordon CMG DSO (XIV-A-13) was a Gordon Highlander officer of many years service who had been wounded at Festubert in May 1915. On 29th July 1917 he was inspecting the assembly trenches of his brigade, 153rd of 51st (Highland) Division, which had been dug for the forthcoming Third Ypres offensive. A shell fell close by killing his Brigade Major, Captain MacLean (See Poperinghe New Military Cemetery – above), and mortally wounded Gordon who died in the 10th CCS on 31st July 1917; just as his men were going over the top. Of the lieutenant colonels, one was the last British officer to die in the Salient. Lieutenant Colonel G.E.Beatty-Pownall DSO (XXX-B-14) died of wounds on 10th October 1918 while commanding 1st Bn King's Own Scottish Borderers.

A Victoria Cross winner is buried here. Major F.H.Tubb VC (XIX-C-5) was one of the first Australians to win the VC. While serving as a Lieutenant in the 7th Bn AIF at Lone Pine, Gallipoli, in August 1915 he repulsed a Turkish counter-attack, despite being seriously wounded in the head and arm. After recovery he returned to the 7th Bn, serving on the Somme and at Ypres, and was mortally wounded in the fighting around Polygon Wood on 20th September 1917.

There are many other interesting characters in the cemetery. Private J.Gaspe (VIII-B-17A) died on 25th June 1916 while serving with the 20th Bn Canadian Infantry. His father was chief of the Iroquois tribe of Canadian Indians'. Captain Atherton Harold Chisenhale-Marsh (XXV-H-27)

**Captain A.H.Chisenhale-Marsh,
9th Lancers.**

139

was an old Etonian who joined the 9th Lancers in 1914 and served with them in the famous charge at Audregnies where Lieutenant Grenfell was awarded the VC (see Vlamtinghe Cemetery in the Behind The Lines Walk). He came to the Salient in 1915 and fought on the Frezenberg Ridge. By 1918 he was a staff officer in the 34th Division and died of wounds received near Kemmel Hill on 28th September 1918. Captain W.A.M.Temple (XXXI-D-19) was the son of Colonel W.Temple VC RAMC who had been awarded the coveted medal in the New Zealand Wars of 1863. Temple junior was a forty-two year old Captain in the 1st Bn Gloucestershire Regiment who died of wounds on 21st October 1914.

Staff Nurse Nellie Spindler (XVI-A-3), of Queen Alexander's Imperial Nursing Service, is the only woman buried at Lijssenthoek. She was killed on 21st August 1917 while attached to 44th CCS at Brandhoek – probably the only woman killed that close to the front at Ypres. The CCS *War Diary* records what happened.

> *Yesterday morning the enemy began to shell the railway alongside the camp and with the third or fourth shell killed S/Nurse N.Spindler. She was hit in the chest and died in about five minutes.*[5]

Four other nurses were concussed by the same shell burst, and as a consequence of these events 44th CCS evacuated all its nurses the next day to St Omer. It also moved back to Remi Sidings, which is where the officers and men from the unit held a burial service for Nurse Spindler. The diary records that during the chaos of the bombardment the Nursing Sisters 'behaved splendidly' and one of them, Sister M.Wood, was subsequently awarded a Military Medal for her bravery that day; one of only a handful of women to win the MM during the Great War.

The buildings of Remi Farm are at the rear of the cemetery. They are on private land and can only be visited with the permission of the owner. British and French graffiti is evident on the farm walls in several places.

1 Williamson, H. *The Wet Flanders Plain* (Faber & Faber 1929) p.36.
2 Town Major Poperinghe *War Diary*, 2.7.15, PRO WO95/4042.
3 Saint-Mande, W. *War, Wine and Women* (Cassell 1931) p.271-273.
4 For further information on executions see Putkowski, J. & Sykes, J. *Shot At Dawn* (Pen & Sword 1989).
5 44th Casualty Clearing Station RAMC *War Diary,* 21.8.17, PRO WO95/345.

Chapter Nine

LOCRE – KEMMEL WALK

STARTING POINT: **Outside Locre church.**
DURATION: **4 hours.**

WALK SUMMARY: *Suitable for the more experienced walker, this walk follows a pleasant route across the Flanders countryside in an area that was behind the lines for most of the war, and climbs Kemmel Hill – one of the highest points on the Ypres battlefield and affording spectacular views of the Salient.*

   Leave your vehicle in one of the parking bays outside Locre (now Loker) church. There are several shops and cafés in the village. War graves in the churchyard are visible to the left of the main entrance.
   Locre was a village located several miles behind the front line after the stalemate of trench warfare set in following First Ypres in 1914. It was a main route up to the trenches in the Messines Ridge sector, and was used for billeting battalions going to and from these positions. RAMC Field Ambulances also set up an Advanced Dressing Station (ADS) here and artillery units had gun sites in the fields and valleys nearby. What had started as a pretty Flemish village was soon turned to rubble by the cruel hand of war. Private Donald Fraser of the 31st Bn Canadian Infantry came to Locre in October 1915 and found it weary after a year of war, but not untypical of many locations behind the lines.

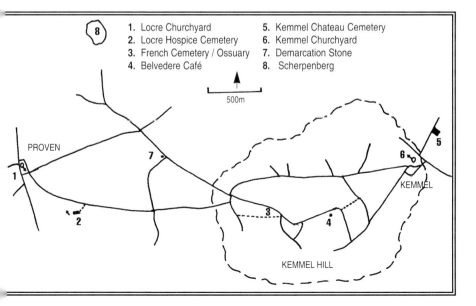

1. Locre Churchyard
2. Locre Hospice Cemetery
3. French Cemetery / Ossuary
4. Belvedere Café
5. Kemmel Chateau Cemetery
6. Kemmel Churchyard
7. Demarcation Stone
8. Scherpenberg

500m

PROVEN

KEMMEL

KEMMEL HILL

Locre in 1914.

The village is dirty and the buildings seem old and unsanitary. The inside of the houses are bare and untidy. What pictures or ornaments there are, are usually emblematic of Catholicism. The people themselves are unkempt. Most of them have a smattering of English picked up from the soldiers and often use swear words not knowing what they mean. The troops air their French which usually amounts to madam, café, compres [sic], oui and a few other words. A conversation between a soldier and a Belgian is very amusing. Every third word is punctuated with 'compres' [sic] and 'oui' with gesticulations.[1]

As the war continued the number of men requiring billets far outstripped the number of suitable buildings in Locre, and around the village vast military camps were constructed, on similar lines to those between Poperinghe and Ypres. Some took the form of huge tented areas, others were more permanent, with wooden buildings or Nissen huts. Each one was named, and marked on trench maps; several here were called after famous battles of the Crimean war. Fighting finally came to Locre in April 1918 when the Germans launched their spring offensive in Flanders, re-capturing Messines Ridge and taking Kemmel Hill. French troops were brought up to support the British, and the line was finally held just outside the village.

LOCRE CHURCHYARD

Burials in the churchyard are split into two plots – one here, and another on the opposite side of the church. It was used by Field Ambulances and fighting units from December 1914 until the Battle of Messines in June 1917. Between the two plots are 184 British and thirty-one Canadian graves; two of them are unknowns. The use of this area by artillery units means that they are well represented; in one row alone are six men of the same artillery battery all killed on the same day in May 1917.

The grave of Second Lieutenant C.Hawdon (I-D-6) records a family tragedy; the inscription reads 'his two brothers also fell. In death they are not divided.' Hawdon died on 27th June 1916, aged twenty-two while serving with the Yorkshire Regiment. His brothers both died in November 1918; one was an army chaplain. In the next row is Bugler J.H.Weatherall (I-E-1) who was killed with 6th Bn Durham Light Infantry on 13th July 1915. The Canadian graves are largely from early 1916, among them two majors buried side by side: Major W.H.Belyea (I-E-12) 26th Bn Canadian Infantry was killed on

The ruins of Locre church, 1915.

20th March 1916, aged thirty-nine. Three days later, on 23rd March, Major W.Bates (I-E-13) of 25th Bn was also killed, and buried here.

Leave this part of the churchyard by the gate and go onto the road in front of the church, turning left and going round to the other side. More war graves are seen at the back.

These are earlier graves from the 1914-15 period and they include many Territorial Force battalions who were amongst the first of the 'Saturday Night Soldiers' to come to Flanders. Among them are burials from, for example, the Honourable Artillery Company and the 10th Bn Liverpool Regiment (Liverpool Scottish), whose medical officer at this time was Captain Noel Chavasse – he later won the VC and bar. A young soldier is Private F.Eke of the Devonshire Regiment who was killed on 28th March 1915, aged sixteen.

Return to the road in front of the church and go left. On the left is the village war memorial. Close by is a French memorial to the 2nd Brigade of Light Cavalry who fought here alongside the British in April 1918. Continue past it and take the first left at the Kemmel sign. Then take the first right down Bergstraat. There are good views towards Kemmel Hill as you come out of the built up area. Continue and then go past a large building resembling a hospital; this is the new Locre Hospice. The site of the original is further along this road, on a bend with a military cemetery in the fields to your right, there is an old

An 'Old Bill Bus' bringing British troops up to the front near Kemmel in 1915.

brick gatepost on the left; now an entrance to a field.

This was the site of the original Locre Hospice: part of the entrance. A large group of brick buildings, one wing was taken over by the RAMC who established an ADS here, which remained in use until 1918. The nuns who lived in the hospice provided meals for British officers during the war, and the complex housed many refuges from Ypres, who made lace while the fighting was going on less than two miles away. Several soldiers were at one time buried in the grounds, but their graves were removed after the war. The Hospice was destroyed by shell fire in April 1918, when it became part of the front line after the Germans captured Kemmel Hill.

Stay on the road; a path to the cemetery soon appears on your right. Follow this to the cemetery.

LOCRE HOSPICE CEMETERY

Started by Field Ambulances, who used Locre Hospice during the Battle of Messines in June 1917, the cemetery remained open until April 1918 when this area became part of the front line. Four graves from the hospice itself were moved here after the war and now there are 255 British burials with two Australian, one Canadian, one New Zealander and two Germans. Two senior officers in the cemetery are: Brigadier General R.C.MacLachlain DSO (II-C-9) of the Rifle Brigade, killed commanding 112th Brigade on 11th August 1917, aged forty-five; a battalion commander is Lieutenant Colonel R.C.Chester-Master DSO and bar, who was killed by a sniper while serving with the 13th Bn King's Royal Rifle Corps on 30th August 1917, aged forty-seven. Known in the regiment as 'The Squire' he was from an old

Gloucestershire family. Chester-Master had commanded the 13th Bn since March 1915, and had served on the Somme, Arras and at Ypres.

A path to the side of the cemetery leads to the isolated grave of Major William Redmond MP. Redmond was a Nationalist Member of Parliament who was really too old for military service but through his contacts had secured a commission in the 6th Bn Royal Irish Regiment. He died of wounds received in the attack on Wytschaete on 7th June 1917, his first major action. Originally his grave was in the garden of Locre Hospice, and it is still flanked by two stones from the old hospice buildings. The grave was moved to this spot after the war and several times the CWGC have requested that it be incorporated into the nearby cemetery, with much resistance from the Redmond family.

Major William Redmond

Return to the road via the grass path and turn right in the direction of Kemmel Hill. At the first crossroads continue straight on, and at the second turn right. Then opposite a building on the right, take a winding track uphill on the left. This brings you to the lower slopes of Kemmel Hill.

Almost at the end of this track, on the left, is an illustrative orientation panel that supplements the commanding view you have from here. Not having reached the summit yet you can already, particularly on a clear day, see as far as Poperinghe and to the south the Lorette spur near Arras and close to Vimy Ridge in France. The importance of high ground in the flatlands of Flanders is very apparent here. Just up the track where it meets the road is the FRENCH OSSUARY. French troops were fighting at Kemmel in April 1918 and this mass grave commemorates 5,294 'Poilus' who died in the 'violent combat around Ypres' as the memorial proclaims. Of this number only fifty-seven are identified. Take time to sign the visitors' book as this cemetery receives few visitors compared to British ones.

From the ossuary gates go straight up the cobbled road ahead of you, which will lead to the crest of Kemmel Hill. On the way is another French memorial to the fighting of April 1918. Follow the road for a

Kemmel hill in 1919.

An old dugout on Kemmel hill, 1919.

few hundred yards to a café-restaurant on the right, noticing signs of trenches and shell holes amongst the trees as you progress.

This is the Belvedere Café, which makes a good stop for liquid refreshment, although meals tend to be a little on the heavy side for most walkers. The huge tower to the rear of the building replaced one that was here before 1914 and was used as an observation post by British officers during the war. On the edge of the car park, in an area clear of trees, is another illustrative orientation panel which overlooks an area from Ypres to Messines.

It was up these slopes that the battle for Kemmel Hill took place in April 1918. During Ludendorff's spring offensive in Flanders the dominating position of Kemmel Hill was one of the key objectives for the Germans. A determined attack on the hill was made on 17th April and repulsed, with a similar story two days later. By this time the German advance appeared to be faltering, and most of the line was handed over to a French Corps which occupied positions from Kemmel to Messines. The 9th (Scottish) Division, however, remained in the sector. On 25th April a further German attack came which swamped the French positions, and at one point the 12th Bn Royal Scots suddenly found German troops 2,000 yards behind their right flank. With the French pushed back, the hill was finally captured. Next day the weary 25th Division made a counter-attack which reached Kemmel village, but the French had failed on their flank and they withdrew. The line settled down between Locre and Kemmel, until American troops from the 27th and 30th (US) Divisions took over the positions here in September 1918. Fighting at that time returned the hill to allied hands.

A wartime view from the summit of Kemmel hill, c.1916.

    From the car park go downhill for a short distance and then turn left onto a track. This is a junction of tracks which run across the hill; take the right hand track, again going downhill. This track eventually meets a minor road; here turn right and then continue until the main road where you turn left and follow it into Kemmel village, and the main square with a bandstand. There are several shops and cafés here; in particular 'Het Labyrint' combines food and drink with a fascinating array of antiques, old toys and archaeological artefacts. It is well worth visiting if you have the time. Also in the main square is the local tourist office.

    Kemmel, like Locre, was a village that remained behind the British

Some of the defenders of Kemmel hill in April 1918: officers and NCOs of the 19th Lancashire Fusiliers. (Salford Pals)

Kemmel village and square in 1914.

lines for most of the war. Nearer the trenches, battalions were billeted in the farms and buildings here, there were headquarters in the main houses and also in a large chateau, set in an elaborate park. Medical units also established an Advanced Dressing Station near the chateau and several cemeteries grew up as a consequence. Thousands of soldiers passed through Kemmel during the Great War, and many have left their impressions of it. In the winter of 1914/15, Captain G.A.Burgoyne spent several months here with the 2nd Bn Royal Irish Rifles. He described a typical billet.

> *The reserve are in a fine farm, the buildings run three sides of a square, in the centre of which is the usual stinking midden and pond. The roof has been blown in over the living rooms, but we occupy the kitchen... We've now installed the Flemish stove taken from the ruined sitting room, and it keeps the room a little warm... The men are in a huge loft, and in the barn on the west side of the square where there is plenty of hay and flax to lie on.'[2]*

He also recalled the village itself at that time.

> *Took a walk around Kemmel town this morning. I don't think that out of a town of some 4,800 inhabitants there is one house quite intact and undamaged by shrapnel, and half the place is in ruins, blown down completely. We passed one building, the front of which is completely wrecked. The wretched occupier has partly blocked up the frameless windows with bricks, above which one can see a shattered interior. However, outside the door hung a pig; inside we saw portions of the other half, a plate of apples and a few other things on sale. There are some dozen shops of sorts where bread, butter, candles, chocolates and sweets... can be bought, and milk and eggs can be easily obtained... The interior of the church is smothered in masonry*

148

dust. A shell has pierced the chancel behind the High Altar and shattered it, and littered the chancel with debris... A lot of the stained glass windows are shattered with shrapnel. It is remarkable that the Christ of the outside wall of the church is quite untouched, though a shell burst at the foot of the cross and the wall all round is pitted with shrapnel.[3]

Spy stories also dominated life in these villages in the early part of the war and Burgoyne noted that in January 1915 two locals were found manipulating the hands of the church clock – seemingly signalling to the Germans – and were discovered by men of the Northumberland Fusiliers who shot them. He also recorded that an officer of the Honourable Artillery Company occupied a billet in Kemmel, which the French had used as a dressing station earlier in the war. One room contained a macabre collection of amputated arms and legs, thrown there in a pile by the orderlies following operations on badly wounded French soldiers.

Despite being behind the lines, Kemmel was often shelled by long-range guns, and on 4th June 1915 two lieutenant colonels became casualties. They were using the old doctor's house as a billet when,

... Colonel Jessop, of the 4th Lincolnshires, was talking to Colonel Jones [5th Leicesters] in the road outside the house, while an orderly held two horses close by. The first shell fell almost on the party, killing Colonel Jessop, the two orderlies... and both horses. Colonel Jones was wounded in the hand, neck and thigh.[4]

Jessop and the orderlies were taken back to Dranoutre for burial, where their graves can be found in the cemetery there.

By the end of 1915 there were fewer civilians in the village, and even more damage to it. The Canadians had by this time taken over the sector east of Kemmel and among them was Private Donald Fraser of the 31st Bn Canadian Infantry who left this description.

Kemmel, in peace time one of the loveliest and most frequented spots in Belgium, was, when we entered it, in a badly battered condition. Still there was quite a number of civilians and several stores were in operation. The town pump, situated in the centre of the square, was intact and from it we replenished our water supply. A fairly elaborate hostel, called the Maison Communale, was doing business as usual; a rather prepossessing young girl of about fifteen dispensing drinks to

Kemmel chateau, 1914.

both soldiers and civilians. Lower down was the Ypres Hotel of doubtful repute. The Brewery, or Brasserie as it is locally called, seemed to be the outstanding industrial establishment though at this time it had ceased activities.[5]

From the main square go south on Polenlaan to a junction opposite a Spar shop. Here turn left and continue to the steps in front of the church; now take the road opposite on the right. This was known as Sackville Street during the war and leads to a military cemetery further up on the right.

Kemmel chateau in ruins with Kemmel Hill in the background

KEMMEL CHATEAU CEMETERY

The original chateau was located in the park to the rear of this cemetery. Owned by the son-in-law of the famous Hennessy brandy family, Private Donald Fraser of the Canadians found it in November 1915 a '... magnificent and imposing turreted building surrounded by a moat, crossed by a little suspension bridge'. During the war it at various stages housed brigade and divisional headquarters, and the RAMC set up an ADS in the chateau grounds. The cemetery was started in December 1914, then used by front line units burying their dead. The RAMC added to it when soldiers died of wounds, as did units in the trenches opposite Wytschaete when they suffered casualties. The cemetery remained in use until March 1918 – the area being taken by the Germans in April – and was partially damaged by shell fire in later fighting. In total there are 1,030 British graves, with eighty Canadian, twenty-four Australian, and one New Zealander.

The cemetery has a distinct 'regimental' feel with, for example, sixty-six graves out of ninety-five in Row E belonging to men of the Sherwood Foresters; largely the 1/8th Bn from April/May 1915. Fifty-eight of the eighty-three soldiers in Row N are from Irish regiments, who are well represented in the whole cemetery. Canadian burials abound in Row K, and the 2nd Bn Royal Scots have a large plot in Row E; eight of them died on 21st April 1915, and one was a seventeen year old soldier, Private A.Darrock (E-17).

There is a very high proportion of officers in this cemetery – with company commanders, adjutants, medical officers and battalion commanders among them. Of the latter, Lieutenant Colonel G.L.B.Du Maurier DSO (L-4) has a well-known name, being an uncle of Daphne Du Maurier. The Colonel died commanding 3rd Bn Royal Fusiliers on 9th March 1915, his death recorded by Captain Burgoyne in his diaries.

Just heard over the telephone from Brigade Head Quarters that Colonel Du Maurier... was killed this morning by a shell which blew up Alston House, the old farm which is always used as Battalion Head Quarters when the Battalion is in the trenches... He was the author of 'An Englishman's Home', the

Kemmel chateau cemetery in 1919.

brother of Gerald Du Maurier and the son of the artist... I hear...
he had just ordered everyone out and into dugouts outside and
was waiting in the house for his Sergeant-Major to report that
everyone was in safety before he took cover himself.[6]

Du Maurier was a long service officer and forty-nine years old when he died. He had fought in both the Burmese and South African wars.

Leaving the cemetery return towards Kemmel via the same road you used to get here. At the end, opposite the church, cross over and climb the steps into the churchyard. The first plots of war graves are to the right of the entrance.

This is KEMMEL CHURCHYARD. You are in the main plot, with graves scattered elsewhere around the church. Most date from 1914/15, with a few of the 1st Gordons from the attack near Wytschaete on 14th December 1914. Among the officers here is Major G.G.P.Humphreys, 127th attached 129th Baluchis Indian Army. He died of wounds received near Hollebeke on 30th October 1914, aged forty-one. Born in Ireland, his grandfather had served under Nelson at Copenhagen, and he had been commissioned in the Welsh Regiment in 1892. Some years later he transferred to the Indian Army and fought in the Uganda Campaign in 1897, with the China Field Force in 1901 and was present at the Delhi Durbar in 1911.

From these graves return towards the main gate you came through, go past it and follow the path round past the civilian graves and the church. Turn left at the Kerkplein sign towards the main square in Kemmel, but as you come out of the churchyard turn sharp right following a Camping sign on the right into Lokerstraat. Follow the road uphill, past the entrance to the campsite, continuing for some

Suicide Corner near Kemmel.

distance until you reach a cross-roads. Here turn right, following a road signposted for Loker, and continue.

Further along on the left where a minor road meets this one is a DEMARCATION STONE. This is one of several placed in the Salient by the Belgian Touring Club in the early 1920s to 'mark the limit of the German invader' as it proclaims. Here the stone denotes where the front lines settled down after the German spring offensive of April 1918. Although in the flatlands below Kemmel Hill, there are good views from here in a north-eastern direction towards Ypres; indeed on a clear day the spires of the Cloth Hall and St Martin's Cathedral can be seen.

Continue from here to another cross-roads. Stop.

Ahead of you in the distance the ground rises to another hill known as the Scherpenberg. As with much of the ground covered by this walk, the Scherpenberg lay behind British lines until April 1918 and there were many hutted camps close by. Indeed, by these cross-roads was the large Sebastopol Camp, and even larger Leeds Camp. On 25th April 1918 the Germans swept down the slopes of Kemmel Hill in an attempt to capture the Scherpenberg, pushing back the French troops who were then holding this sector. However, the French 39th Division stopped the Germans and the hill was held; the valley between it and Kemmel becoming No Man's Land until September 1918.

At the cross-roads turn left and follow a long straight road back to Locre. This last part of the journey I find very evocative; this road is so typical of the routes to and from the back areas of Flanders. How many battalions marched up this road to the line, and how many men marched back again afterwards? With these thoughts in mind Locre is soon reached. The road comes into the village at the rear of the churchyard; follow it round to the front of the church and your vehicle.

1 Roy, R.H. (Ed) *The Journal of Private Fraser* (Sono Nis Press 1985) p.37-38.
2 Burgoyne, G.A. *The Burgoyne Diaries* (Thomas Harmsworth 1985) p.47.
3 ibid. p.114-115.
4 Hills, J.D. *The Fifth Leicestershire: A Record of the 1/5th Battalion the Leicestershire Regiment TF during the War 1914-1919* (Echo Press 1919) p.34.
5 Roy op cit. p.49.
6 Burgoyne op cit. p.135-139.

All that was left of Locre in 1918.

Chapter Ten

'WHITESHEET' WALK

STARTING POINT: **Wytschaete Military Cemetery.**
DURATION: **3¹/₂ hours.**

WALK SUMMARY: *An easy walk covering the positions on the Messines Ridge around the village of Wytschaete, known as 'Whitesheet' to British troops. It links well with the Messines Ridge Walk and an experienced walker might even consider doing them together as one long walk.*

Wytschaete, or Wijtschate as it is known today, is just off the main Ypres – Armentieres road and the military cemetery is just outside the western edge of the village on the route to Kemmel. A parking area in front of the cemetery provides a suitable area to leave your vehicle.

The ruins of Wytschaete after its capture. TAYLOR LIBRARY

WYTSCHAETE MILITARY CEMETERY

No cemetery existed on this site during the war, and all these graves were brought in from burial sites in a wide area about the Messines Ridge, and indeed other parts of the Salient. Today it contains 486 British graves, along with thirty-one Australian, nineteen Canadian, eleven South African, seven New Zealand and one German. Of these 423 are unknown; the vast majority of the burials here. Twenty-five Special Memorials commemorate men whose graves were lost.

Close by the cemetery is the memorial to the 16th (Irish) Division. Raised in 1914 from New Army battalions of southern Irish regiments, it had fought with distinction at Guillemont and Ginchy in 1916. During the Battle of Messines in June 1917 it fought alongside the 36th (Ulster) Division in the capture of Wytschaete. Another memorial to this division, of the same design, exists at Guillemont on the Somme.

Leave the cemetery by the main gate and turn right, following the Kemmel road westwards. It is advisable to keep on the right-hand side of the road in the cycle lane – although beware of cyclists who can

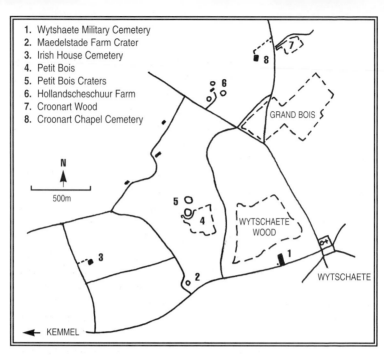

1. Wytshaete Military Cemetery
2. Maedelstade Farm Crater
3. Irish House Cemetery
4. Petit Bois
5. Petit Bois Craters
6. Hollandscheschuur Farm
7. Croonart Wood
8. Croonart Chapel Cemetery

N

500m

GRAND BOIS

WYTSCHAETE WOOD

WYTSCHAETE

KEMMEL

approach from either direction! As you come out of the village boundary, past some modern houses, the trees surrounding Spanbroekmolen mine crater can be seen to the left (see Messines Ridge Walk). Further along turn right at the Oosthoeve signboard down Klein Wijtschaete Str to the area known as Maedelstade Farm on British maps.

Maedelstade Farm was a farm complex west of the road you are on – roughly on the site of the present day buildings – which formed part of the German lines here on this sector of the Messines Ridge. No Man's Land was about 300 yards across here, and a network of

The ruins of 'Whitesheet' in 1919.

trenches had grown up around the farm since the lines stabilised in the winter of 1914. On high ground, Maedelstade Farm afforded good views across to the British trenches and beyond to the rear areas towards Kemmel. All the German lines in this sector had names beginning with N, and Nap Trench protected the ruins of the farm buildings. Infantry assaults earlier in the war had proved this a formidable defensive work and by 1916, when plans for an attack on the Messines Ridge were being formulated, it was decided that this would be an area to use one of the mines which would open the attack.

Major Cropper's 250th Tunnelling Company Royal Engineers were brought in to this sector to prepare this and the other mines for Messines; from Hollandscheschuur Farm to Peckham – the largest area covered by a single Tunnelling Company. The tunnel towards Maedelstade Farm was started in 1916, but the final charges, amounting to 94,000lbs of explosive (a mixture of Ammonal and gun cotton), were still being laid as late as 2nd June 1917 – only five days before the battle was due to start. The gallery leading to the main charge was over 1,600 feet long, a hundred feet below ground at its greatest depth and was designed to explode behind the farm buildings on a spot where a network of trenches was located. A second gallery, branching off from the main one, had been directed towards Wytschaete Wood, but lack of time prior to the battle meant this ambitious plan had to be abandoned.

On 7th June 1917, the 16th (Irish) Division occupied this part of the line, alongside their comrades in the 36th (Ulster) Division on the right; the first time these two formations had fought side by side. At 3.10am the mines used on this front were blown using detonators or electricity, and at Maedelstade Farm a smoking crater 205 feet across was made. The total area of destruction was more than another hundred feet around this. Units from Brigadier General Pereira's 47th Brigade then attacked the farm; the shock of the mine explosions here and at Petit Bois and Peckham broke the back of the German defences and the position was easily captured. From here the Irishmen pushed on into Wytschaete Wood and the village itself.

Today Maedelstade Farm crater is still impressive, but lies in private land used for fishing competitions and is often closed off from public access during the winter months. Opposite is a café with an information panel in Flemish and English about the area, and refreshments can be bought here; although opening times seem to vary.

From the café continue along the road – Klein Wijtschaete Str – as it moves north from the craters and past a farm on the right. Just past

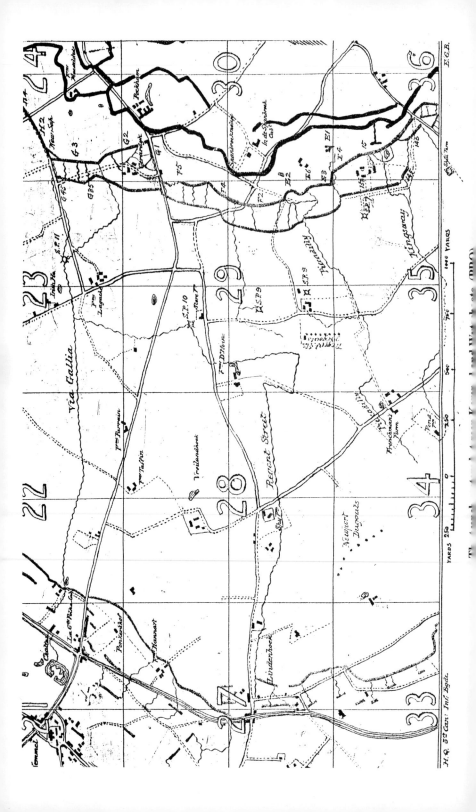

H.Q. 3rd Can: Inf: Bgde.

YARDS 250   0   250   500   750   1000 YARDS

E.G.B.

the farm is your first view to the right towards Petit Bois. Continue through a partially sunken area and take the first minor road on the left – Maedelstadestraat – then on the rise turn round to view Petit Bois. Stop.

Going north along the Messines Ridge, Petit Bois, a small wood (thus its name) incorporated into the German front line was the next key objective in this sector for the fighting on 7th June 1917. Opposite the British trenches on Vandamme Hill, Nancy Trench constituted the German forward positions and mining activity had already begun as early as 1915 – several small craters littered No Man's Land. In early 1916 Major Cropper's 250th Tunnelling Company began work here and constructed a gallery with two branches each of which would eventually contain charges of 30,000lbs of explosive. Unique to the tunnellers who worked on the Messines Ridge, Major Cropper had brought up a mechanical mining machine similar to those used in constructing underground railway tunnels in England. It was an impressive piece of equipment.

> *The machine consisted of a chassis on wheels carrying a pair of rotating cutters at the front. These cutters were powered by a two-cylinder compressed air engine which was in turn driven by a miniature generating station installed on the surface. As the compressed air blasted into the cutters they screwed themselves forward tearing out the face ahead and feeding the spoil back. While cutting went on the machine was stabilised by top and bottom jacks.*[1]

The cutter was broken down into its component parts and taken piece by piece down a narrow shaft, and assembled in the mining gallery. The heavy sections were brought up at night by trench railway, but it soon became impossible to disguise that work was going on and the German artillery began to concentrate fire on the positions near the shaft entrance. Wild rumours – beloved of all soldiers in any war – began to circulate and there was much speculation that this was a secret, war-winning weapon which had been brought up to clear the Germans off the Messines Ridge in one go. After final assembly it was first used on 4th March 1916, and the initial results were good. However, after it was turned off for maintenance it failed to re-start and Cropper discovered the machine had entangled itself in the clay and had to be dug free. This continued to happen each time it was operated and a catalogue of mechanical problems eventually led to the 'secret weapon' being abandoned after it had only cut 200 feet of tunnel. This gallery was then sealed up and abandoned – and the machine lies there to this day, eighty or more feet below the surface; although there is talk in Ypres of having it excavated.

The Petit Bois craters are visible from here with a good pair of binoculars – they appear as indents in the ground from this angle, and are surrounded by several small trees. On private land the craters cannot be visited, but will be seen more clearly later on in the walk.

Turning round again, continue along Maedelstadestraat to where it joins another road and here turn right. Continue past the farm to a gate opening on to a grass path across the field to a military cemetery.

IRISH HOUSE CEMETERY

Irish House was the name given by British troops to the original of the farm building you have just passed. The cemetery was started after the Messines offensive in June 1917 when units of the 16th (Irish) Division buried their dead here. It remained in use until September 1918, falling into German hands in April that year. There are 103 British burials, and fourteen Australian. Several artillery graves reflect the nature of this position and the use of the natural valley in which the cemetery is located – an ideal gun site out of view of German positions on and beyond Messines Ridge.

After the Battle of Messines, 11th Bn Royal Irish Rifles cleared this part of the battlefield and discovered the remains of a large group of Gordon Highlanders who had been lying in No Man's Land since their deaths in December 1914. The thirty-three officers and men recovered and buried in a mass grave at Irish House (A-30/32) were from 1st Gordons, part of 3rd Division, who had been killed in an ill thought out attack near Wytschaete on 14th December 1914. The battalion *War Diary* records the following account of what happened.

At 7am our artillery bombardment commences. Many of our shells fell short of the German position, some even in rear of our reserve.

At 7.45am... [we] advanced from the fire trenches and pushed on in extended order in spite of very heavy rifle fire which was immediately opened on us. The sodden nature of the ground and the fact that the men had been standing for several hours in trenches deep in mud rendered a rapid advance impossible.

The heavy rifle and machine-gun fire which was opened from the German trenches showed at once that the artillery bombardment had failed in its purpose and that the German trenches were still strongly held. Many casualties occurred as our men left the trenches but the advance was not checked. The attacking companies soon disappeared from view and in default of any means of communication with them it was impossible to tell how they were progressing.[2]

The 1st Gordons had managed at one point to enter the German positions, but were in isolated groups up and down the line. Slowly these groups were pushed back, overwhelmed or taken prisoner, and by the close of the fighting that day the battalion had lost seventeen officers and 253 men – over 50% casualties. As trench warfare settled down to stalemate, the bodies of the Gordons could not be recovered and were left. Units in and out of the line could see them and do nothing. Many speculated as to their fate, and as time progressed, stories abounded as to what had happened here. Captain G.A.Burgoyne of the 2nd Bn Royal Irish Rifles reported in January 1915,

> *... one of our MG section was telling me of the charge of the Gordons made on December 14th... An officer drew his claymore, yelled 'Advance' and they were up and out over the poor parapets, and went real well. One young NCO he noticed, galloping ahead, his rifle in the air, yelling 'Come on boys'... he pointed out to me what he thought was the poor boy's body, not 50 yards from the German lines... Our guns were pouring heavy shrapnel fire into the German lines and many poor Highlanders were knocked over by our own shrapnel... The whole affair was apparently very badly organised; never thought out at all. But then the whole time I have been out I never once saw any of our Brigade or Divisional staff come up to the trenches.*[3]

Nearly a year after the action, in November 1915, the bodies were still lying there and were noticed by Private Donald Fraser of the 31st Bn Canadian Infantry; he took special interest as he himself was a Scot by birth and instantly recognised these kilted troops as fellow countrymen. While exploring No Man's Land at night, Fraser and his comrades discovered,

> *... a fairly even line of dead three or four hundred yards long... Most of the bodies were skeletons or partly mummified and fell to pieces when moved. Some were half buried. One Highlander was fairly intact. On two of them we found paybooks, a watch and some money. Their names were Robb and Anderson, and they belonged to Aberdeen, Scotland. Robb was married and had several letters in his possession. There was one written by*

himself to his wife. Of course it was never posted. It was dated...
December 1914. He was very optimistic regarding the war, went
even as far as to say it would be finished in a week or two, and
expected to be home for Xmas. His paybook had only one entry,
a payment made in October. He was clothed in winter garb and
had his equipment over a light coloured goatskin. He was lying
facing the German line and his rifle, with bayonet fixed, was
lying about a foot to his right.[4]

One can only imagine the state the bodies were in when they were
eventually laid to rest by 11th Royal Irish Rifles in June 1917 – indeed
it is a miracle that any bodies had survived to bury. Only three of the
thirty-three are known – the unknowns all marked by one unique
headstone. Those whose identity could be ascertained were Lieutenant
W.R.F.Dobie (A-30), Lieutenant J.J.G.MacWilliam (A-30) and CQMS
A.McKinley (A-31). MacWilliam was a nineteen-year-old subaltern
from Edinburgh who had joined the battalion in September 1914, and
had already been wounded at La Bassée in October. One of his men
wrote to MacWilliam's parents after the action describing what had
happened to their son.

When the order came to advance he was the first out of the
trenches. Smiling and waving his stick, he encouraged his men
on. When he had got to within fifty yards of the German trenches
we had to lie down for a minute to get our breath before making
the final assault. It was when he raised his head to give the order
to advance that he was killed.[5]

Leave the cemetery by the same path and returning to the road turn
right and continue. At the end of this road turn right. Further on, as the
road climbs uphill, it forks; take the left-hand fork towards a farm on
Mandesstraat. Go past the farm (Vandamme Farm on British maps),
and then further on by a new house on the right where the road bends
– stop.

From here you have a good view towards the trees of Petit Bois. The
edges of the craters are just visible – small stumpy trees can be seen
growing round the lips of them. From left to right the view here takes
in Hollandscheschuur Farm, Croonart Wood, Grand Bois, Unnamed
Wood and Petit Bois, with Wytschaete Wood and the spire of
Wytschaete church beyond.

Work on the Petit Bois mines had started in December 1915. Six
months later in June 1916, as the work progressed, German tunnellers
blew two counter-mines which caved in 250 yards of the workings.

A German front line trench near Petit Bois.

Twelve Sappers were entombed at the German end, cut off from their comrades by the fall-in. A rescue party laboured ten days to get them out and,

> ... when at last they got through they discovered the bodies of the imprisoned men, who had collected near the block to listen for the sounds of the rescue work, and had all been suffocated, as this point, happening to be the lowest, was a pit of foul air. But one man, a miner by trade, had stayed in a higher part of the

gallery, and he was found alive. He owed his life to finding half
a pint of water in a bottle, which he kept taking into his mouth
and returning to the flask.[6]

Despite this setback, the two mines designated for this sector were completed by August 1916, each containing a charge of 30,000 lbs. Brigadier General P.Leveson-Gower's 49th Brigade of the 16th (Irish) Division successfully attacked and captured Petit Bois on the morning of 7th June 1917. The Official History reports that these mines were fired twelve seconds late, causing casualties in the leading battalions and blowing many men off their feet, as at Spanbroekmolen nearby (See Messines Ridge Walk).

Continue along this road until it meets the main Vierstraat – Wytschaete road. At this junction stop and look up the sloping ground towards Hollandscheschuur Farm.

Hollandscheschuur Farm stands on a high point overlooking this part of the battlefield and was fortified by the Germans as part of their defences in this sector of the Messines Ridge. Three mines were started in December 1915, and completed between June and August 1916. No 1 Mine was a charge of 34,200 lbs, and the others 14,900 and 18,500 respectively. On 7th June 1917 the 56th Brigade of 19th (Western) Division attacked across this ground, greatly assisted by the explosions which neutralised the German garrison. The divisional *War Diary* records, '... there was little resistance from the Germans, who either ran forward to surrender, or, if they could do so, ran away; very few of them put up a fight.'[7]

Follow the main road uphill in the direction of Wytschaete. The main entrance to Hollandscheschuur Farm is passed on the left, but this is private and access to the mine craters cannot be gained without permission of the owners. Just before Grand Bois there is a minor road to the left, Kroonaardstraat. Stop here before taking this route and look back – there is a good view from the German perspective towards the British positions you have just walked across. Follow Kroonaardstraat to the end and turn left on the outskirts of Grand Bois towards another wood which is soon reached on the right.

Croonart Wood, or Bois Quarante (from when the French held this sector), formed part of the German line from October 1914 until captured in the Battle of Messines. It was part of the Salient Adolf Hitler knew well, having been awarded an Iron Cross 2nd Class near here in 1914, and then later returned to the wood in 1916. On 7th June 1917 this was part of the attack area of Major General Shute's 19th (Western) Division, and men of the 9th Bn Cheshire Regiment were

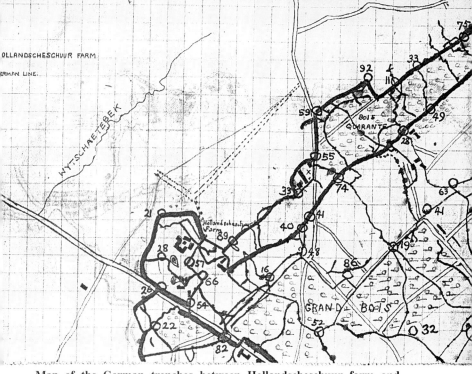

Map of the German trenches between Hollandscheschuur farm and Croonart Wood.

present in the attack on the wood itself. For many years Croonart Wood was a trench museum similar to Sanctuary Wood, and run by the enterprising Andre Becquart. It was interesting as it showed the contrast between the German trenches here and the British at Sanctuary Wood. A larger section of the front line could be explored with mine craters, shell holes, concrete bunkers and a mine shaft which at one time visitors could be winched up and down in a bucket seat. On display were a wide variety of battlefield relics, including human skulls which adorned Andre's front room window - still wearing Picklehaubes! A great storyteller, Andre claimed that Hitler had been wounded here in 1916 and placed in a concrete bunker to await evacuation. Later that night there was a British trench raid, and a British officer entered the trench, saw the bunker and pulled back the gas blanket and made his way inside. There he found the pathetic figure of the wounded Hitler, lying on a stretcher. Levelling his revolver the officer paused for a moment and on reflection said, 'I won't shoot you, you'll do no harm.' It is one of those stories the truth of which is lost to history itself, although Andre certainly did have photographs of Hitler returning to Croonart Wood in May 1940. Sadly the wood was abandoned after Andre's death in the mid-1980s, and its fate still remains unknown. It is private property, and should not be entered; many of the old trenches and the mine shaft are now very dangerous. However, from the edge of it, where a minor road runs along its main length, there are good views across the battlefield where the 19th Division fought in June 1917.

From the wood go downhill slightly until a grass path is found on the left. Follow this to the cemetery.

CROONART CHAPEL CEMETERY

A small battlefield cemetery of seventy-four British graves, with one man of the Chinese Labour Corps, it was begun in June 1917 by burial officers of the 19th Division. Soldiers from several units of that division are found here, but it stayed in use until November 1917, with two graves being added in April 1918. The small, now heavily weathered, French memorial by the access path is to Lieutenant Lasnier and his comrades of the 1st Battalion Light Infantry (Chasseurs à Pied) who died in this sector in 1914.

Return via the grass path to the road. Turn right and go back past Croonart Wood to Kroonaardstraat on the outskirts of Grand Bois. Follow it back to the Vierstraat road and turn right, then immediate left on another minor road. This road goes uphill as it climbs the slopes of the Messines Ridge and passes a modern house on the left. Just past this, stop. There are good views down towards the Petit Bois craters and here, perhaps more than anywhere else on this walk, it is quite apparent how important a feature the Messines Ridge was – the field of vision even on a dull day is considerable.

Continue as the road passes between Wytschaete Wood and Petit Bois. At the end it meets the Kemmel road. Here turn left and stay on the cycle path back to the cemetery and your vehicle.

1 Barrie, A. *War Underground* (House Journals 1964) p.183.
2 1st Bn Gordon Highlanders *War Diary*, 14.12.14, PRO WO95/1421.
3 Burgoyne, G.A. *The Burgoyne Diaries* (Thomas Harmsworth 1985) p.50-51.
4 Roy, R.H. *The Journal of Private Fraser* (Sono Nis Press 1985) p.55.
5 Quoted in Clutterbuck, L.A. (Ed) *The Bond of Sacrifice* Volume I (Anglo-African Publishing 1915) p.248.
6 Brice, B. *The Battle Book of Ypres* (John Murray 1927) p.169-170.
7 Quoted in Edmonds, J.E. (Ed) *Military Operations France and Belgium 1917* Volume II (HMSO 1948) p.59.

Chapter Eleven

MESSINES RIDGE WALK

STARTING POINT: **St Quentin Cabaret Military Cemetery, Wulverghem.**
DURATION· **7 hours** [excluding extra time spent in Messines].

WALK SUMMARY: *This is the longest walk in the book, and is best spread over the course of a day. However, it is one of the most rewarding as most of the route is off road and down tracks. The views of Messines and the ridge itself are also quite staggering at times.*

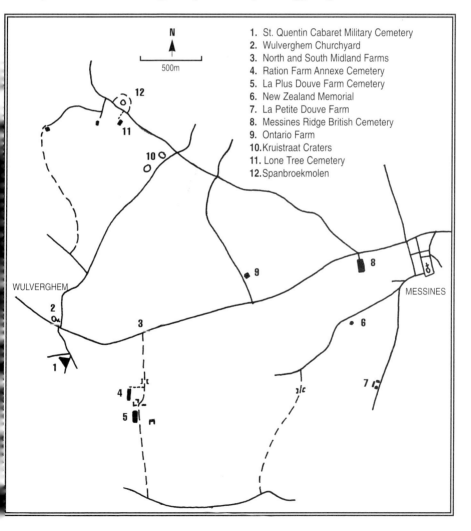

1. St. Quentin Cabaret Military Cemetery
2. Wulverghem Churchyard
3. North and South Midland Farms
4. Ration Farm Annexe Cemetery
5. La Plus Douve Farm Cemetery
6. New Zealand Memorial
7. La Petite Douve Farm
8. Messines Ridge British Cemetery
9. Ontario Farm
10. Kruistraat Craters
11. Lone Tree Cemetery
12. Spanbroekmolen

St Quentin Cabaret Military Cemetery is on a minor road going south from the centre of Wulverghem, and is clearly signposted. There is ample parking outside the cemetery, with plenty of room to leave your vehicle.

ST QUENTIN CABARET MILITARY CEMETERY

St Quentin Cabaret was the name given to an old Flemish inn 500 yards east of Kandahar Farm on the south side of Wulverghem, and whose cellars were used as a battalion headquarters and aid post during the Great War. The building is opposite the cemetery, and is now a private house. Units in the line opposite Messines in the River Douve sector knew it well and the nearby military cemetery was started by battalions of the 46th (North Midland) Division who came to this area in February 1915; Plot I, Rows E and F contain these early graves. The cemetery remained in use until 1918, although only two graves were added after September 1918 when the area was re-captured from the Germans after their spring offensive in April. There are 316 British burials, of which eighty are men from the 36th (Ulster) Division, with sixty-eight Canadian, sixty-four New Zealand, seven Australian, two German and five whose unit is not known.

The graves from early 1915 are largely men in the 1/5th and 1/6th Bns South Staffordshire Regiment, but among them is that of a soldier who fell at Messines in 1914. Pte J.W.Bremner (I-G-11) died with the 2nd Bn Royal Scots on 16th November 1914, but the placing of his grave and history of the cemetery suggests that his body was found on the battlefield many months later and buried here by the Staffordshire territorials.

Among the Canadian graves in Plot I, Row C, are a row of eighteen men of 1st Bn Canadian Infantry, all of whom died on 13th October 1915. Holding the line opposite Petit Douve Farm their battalion *War Diary* records a typical episode in the day to day activity of trench warfare in this sector – and the fate of these eighteen men.

> *Brigade made a demonstration consisting of artillery bombardment and feint attack with smoke bombs. Heavy retaliation by enemy artillery caused casualties. Killed, 18, wounded, 26. Trenches suffered considerable damage. Behaviour of troops admirable, though many of them had not been under serious shell fire before.*

Two long serving officers are elsewhere in the cemetery. Major D.D.H.Campbell MC (II-J-5) was killed in action with 112th Brigade

RFA in the opening phase of Messines on 7th June 1917, aged thirty-three. The son of a lieutenant colonel, he had previously fought in the Mohmand Campaign in 1908 with the Native Mountain Artillery, and 1913-14 with the Burma Police. He was the sixth generation of his family to see military service. Lieutenant-Quartermaster J.Bowyer MC (II-E-8) was killed two days later on 9th June, aged fifty. An old soldier who had been commissioned from the ranks, Bowyer was an original member of 11th Bn Lancashire Fusiliers, having been their quartermaster since the formation of the unit in 1914. He was awarded the Military Cross for bravery near Le Sars on the Somme in 1916.

The eighty graves of men from the 36th (Ulster) Division in Plot I date from when the formation left the Somme after their blooding at Thiepval on 1st July 1916; the Ulstermen suffered over 5,500 casualties that day. Many of those buried here had survived these operations only to be killed in a 'quiet' sector. Among them was the adjutant of 10th Bn Royal Irish Rifles, Captain J.E.Sugden DSO (I-D-13). Sugden had been commissioned in 1914, promoted adjutant by the Somme, and awarded his Distinguished Service Order for bravery at Thiepval. He was killed by a shell on 28th September 1916, aged thirty-eight.

Leaving the cemetery gates turn left and take the minor road leading to Wulverghem. This will soon bring you into the centre of the village and to a crossroads with the church opposite. Cross the road to the churchyard, where there are a number of war graves. It is entered by some steps and a gate.

Wulverghem is a small village west of Messines Ridge which remained behind British lines for most of the war, until the area was swept up in the German offensive in April 1918. Used as a billet for troops going to and from the line in the Petit Douve sector, many of the cellars were taken over as dugouts. Artillery units also established gun sites around the village, in the many hidden valleys out of view of the German trenches and they, too, had their billets here. Gradually, through constant shell fire, the village was destroyed and completely rebuilt after the war. A few burials were made in the churchyard in 1914/15, but once a proper Advanced Dressing Station was made at St Quentin Cabaret, a military cemetery was established there.

Bruce Bairnsfather, creator of the 'Old Bill' cartoons, came to Wulverghem in late 1914, with the 1st Bn Royal Warwickshire Regiment.

The village street is one long ruin. On either side of the road all the houses are merely a collection of broken tiles and

shattered bricks and framework. Huge shell holes puncture the street. The church... was a large reddish-grey stone building, pretty old, and surrounded by a graveyard. Shell holes everywhere; the old grey grave stones and slabs cracked and sticking about at odd angles.

Not a soul about anywhere. Wulverghem lay there, empty, wrecked and deserted.

WULVERGHEM CHURCHYARD consists of one plot of Special Memorials to soldiers who are known to be buried here but the exact location of the grave is now lost – the church and churchyard were heavily shelled in April 1918. Only two headstones mark original graves – those of two unknown soldiers of the 1/9th Bn London Regiment (Queen Victoria's Rifles). The thirty-two Special Memorials commemorate a variety of units which served in the Wulverghem area between October 1914 and April 1915.

Bruce Bairnsfather in trench kit, 1914.

Among them is a Squadron Sergeant Major, H.W.Baker (B-2), of 11th Hussars who was killed on the Messines Ridge on 30th October 1914, aged thirty-six. A typical 'old sweat', he had twenty years service in the army.

Leaving the churchyard by the same gate where you came in, turn left on the main road and follow it in the direction of Messines. The road soon bends, and climbs uphill. In the uncultivated field on the left there are signs of shell-holes among the grass. Continue on this road until it reaches a set of buildings   with a white farmhouse on the right.

The farms left and right of this road were known as North and South Midland Farms respectively on British trench maps, presumably acquiring their names from when the 46th (North Midland) and 48th (South Midland) Divisions were in this sector in early 1915. There are good views towards the Messines Ridge, with the trees surrounding Spanbroekmolen mine crater on the left and Messines itself straight ahead. The importance of this high ground, and the way in which it clearly dominated the battlefield, are quite apparent.

At the white building on your right (South Midland Farm), and by a CWGC sign for Ration Farm Cemetery, take a minor road going downhill into the Douve valley. Follow this until it reaches a small bridge. Stop.

This is the Douve River. Using the trench map below, it is possible to plot the whole extent of the line in this sector, as all the farms destroyed during the war were rebuilt and the ground itself has changed little. It gives a good impression of how a battalion operated in the Salient during the quiet times between major actions. In the far distance La Petite Douve Farm is visible on the slopes of Messines Ridge – this was the German front line. Short of that the British trenches can be plotted using the map. Here the positions would be held by one or two companies of whichever battalion was in the line at a given date. A second company would be in reserve between Fort Hambury and Fort Stewart, with advanced company headquarters in Stinking Farm. The officer commanding the front line company would be in La Plus Douve or Ration Farm (now just ahead of you), as would be the ration parties, signallers, runners and the reserve company. Telephone lines, which needed constant attention during periods of heavy shelling, would link up all these positions and allow communication. Further back at St Quentin Cabaret (also visible from the bridge) was battalion headquarters, where the commanding officer, second in command, adjutant and medical officer had a dugout in the cellar. The battalion cookers were also located there, and at night fatigue parties would bring up tea and stew to Ration Farm, and then, via communication trenches such as Calgary Avenue, to the men in the

The trench system in the Petit Douve valley. (PRO)

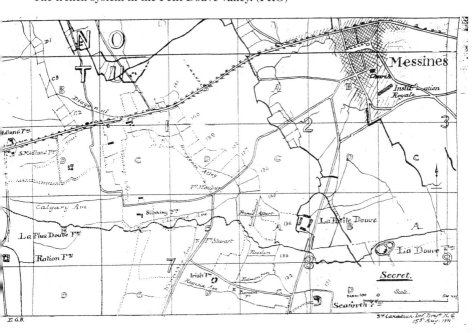

front line. Such arrangements would continue for days at a time, with companies rotating back and forth between reserve and forward positions until another battalion relieved them and they would move back, usually via Wulverghem, to a village or rest camp well out of shell range. One sector on one part of the Western Front, this routine was repeated many times over all along the line from Ypres to the Somme and beyond.

Continue on the track to a CWGC sign and take the grass path on the right to the cemetery.

RATION FARM ANNEXE (LA PLUS DOUVE) CEMETERY

The cemetery was started in January 1915 close to the farm complex known on trench maps as La Plus Douve Farm, and remained in use for a further three years until January 1918. No further graves were added after this date – all local burials were then made at La Plus Douve Cemetery nearby. It contains 186 British burials, twelve Australian, four New Zealand, one German prisoner, and one whose unit could not be identified.

Started by the 2nd Bn Manchester Regiment, Private H.Bates (I-A-8) was the first burial on 11th January 1915, when he was killed. Most graves are from the 1915-16 period, with a few in 1917 and the last being made by Australian units in January 1918. The cemetery is dominated by Irish regiments; largely battalions of the 36th (Ulster) Division from August – September 1916 after their heavy losses at Thiepval on 1st July 1916. There are also some men of the 2nd Bn Leinster Regiment, from 24th Division, who were here in early 1916. Among these are two drummers: M.Morrissey (II-C-17) who died on 5th April 1916 and A.Murphy (II-C-13) killed 17th April 1916. Indeed there are many 24th Division graves in the cemetery, including a large plot of 9th Bn Royal Sussex Regiment men who died on 17th June 1916, when the Germans heavily gassed the British trenches, causing several casualties. The last soldier to be interred here was Private V.T.Stone MM (III-B-19), 12th Bn AIF, who is recorded as having drowned on 16th January 1918; possibly in the Douve River?

Leave the cemetery by the path, and at the end turn right. Go through the farmyard and take the track to the cemetery on the right.

LA PLUS DOUVE FARM CEMETERY

The Douve river ran through two large farms – La Plus Douve and La Petite Douve – the latter scene of a large Canadian trench raid in November 1915 and where one of the Messines mines was discovered

172

by the Germans in 1916. You have just passed through La Plus Douve; La Petite Douve is further down the valley and will be seen later. This cemetery, which complemented the one you have just come from, was started in April 1915 by units of the 48th (South Midland) Division, and stayed in use until May 1918; latterly by the Germans who captured the ground in April. It has 101 British, eighty-eight Canadian, eighty-six Australian, sixty-one New Zealand and nine German graves.

The Canadian graves date from 1915 and are all 1st Division men who held this sector after the fighting near Kitchener's Wood and St Julien, during Second Ypres. Elsewhere is an Englishman who had emigrated to America, Private R.Knight Cuthbert of 2nd King Edward's Horse, one of several men from this unit buried here, who was forty-seven when he was killed on 7th July 1915. The inscription on his headstone reads, 'From America he came on homeland's duty call'. New Zealand graves date from the Messines offensive in 1917, and the Australians from February and March 1918.

Leaving the cemetery turn right and continue on the track. At the end it meets a road; here turn left and follow. Further along on the crest are good views. From here you can see, left to right: Kemmel Hill, Spanbroekmolen, Wytschaete Wood, Wytschaete, Messines Ridge, the New Zealand Memorial and Messines itself (distinguished by the church tower). Continue. Further along, between two farms and just before a bend to the right there is a track to the left going downhill towards Messines. Stop here before following this track.

There are good views towards Messines and the area of operations of the New Zealand Division (see map). The NZ Division was one of the most disciplined and highly respected fighting formations in the British Expeditionary Force, and many of its men had fought at Gallipoli in 1915, and near High Wood on the Somme in 1916.

A British tank knocked out on Messines ridge.

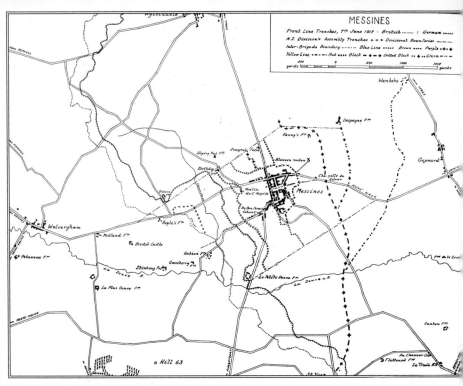

Map showing the New Zealand Division area of operations, 7th June 1917.

Messines Ridge was to prove one of their most successful operations, despite what appears to be almost impossible odds and terrain. No mines were used on their immediate divisional front – the one at La Petite Douve having been discovered by the Germans in 1916 – and the slopes of the ridge were particularly steep, making movement up them difficult. The Germans had constructed a strong defence line around Messines itself, with many concrete bunkers. However, following a very well planned and executed preliminary bombardment, and the construction of assembly trenches in No Man's Land, therefore reducing the distance men had to advance, the attack went well. The explosion of the Ontario mine on the left flank (25th Division front) signalled the advance, and the New Zealanders left their trenches. There was no creeping barrage to protect them as they crossed No Man's Land, but a fixed 18-pounder bombardment of the German front line neutralised the garrison as the Kiwis advanced. They soon reached the enemy positions, and as the shell fire lifted from the German trenches they were in at the point of the bayonet. The ground was soon swept up and within forty minutes the New Zealanders were in Messines itself, clearing dugouts and taking prisoners. On their left the

25th Division had come forward and taken their objectives, the 3rd (Australian) Division doing the same on the right. Messines Ridge had been captured. All this was achieved with minimal casualties for a Great War battle, and the ridge was held against counter-attacks.

Follow the track downhill. In wet weather it can be boggy or flooded, and it might be necessary to walk along the edge of a field in several places. The track brings you down to another bridge over the Douve river. Stop here and look east, towards a farm building astride the Ypres – Armentieres road.

This is La Petite Douve Farm, a bastion in the German lines which overlooked the British trenches in the Douve valley. In November 1915 the 7th Bn Canadian Infantry had organised a large trench raid on the position, but it had remained in enemy hands. When plans for the Battle of Messines were being formulated in 1916, the farm was selected as a suitable target for one of the offensive mines, and men of 171st Tunnelling Company RE were allocated to prepare the mine. In August 1916 German sappers, who were counter-mining at the same time, broke into the main shaft and attempted to remove the thirty-five ton charge. But the REs were aware of their activities and exploded a camouflet, killing the enemy miners. Several days later the Germans retaliated with a 6,000 lb charge which severely damaged the tunnel, and the officers in command were then in favour of blowing the mine. However, they were overruled; La Petite Douve was abandoned and the course of the Douve River directed into the tunnel, flooding the workings of both sides.

Continue along the track; it soon meets a minor road and stay on this until you cross a stream. Here you are on the approximate New Zealand front line for 7th June 1917, with the German lines on the high ground ahead of you; they were just in front of the New Zealand Memorial, and the bunkers, which formed part of it, are just visible on a clear day. It is very obvious here just how the Germans dominated the British positions in the Douve valley. Stay on this road and follow it uphill. Further along on the left is a small wayside shrine; stop and look back across the ground you have just walked. It gives a good impression of the German view down into the valley. One of the front line bunkers is seen in a nearby field on your right.

A little further up the slope is the NEW ZEALAND MEMORIAL. This is a large Portland stone memorial commemorating the capture of the ridge in June 1917, which was unveiled by King Albert of the Belgians on 1st August 1924. Part of a park, in the grounds are two German bunkers which can be easily explored. They, too, afford good views down to the former British lines. An inscription on the memorial records that these Kiwis came 'from the uttermost ends of the earth', and paid a high price. By 1918 New Zealand, with a population of 1,099,449 had raised 128,525 men to fight in the war. Of these 100,440 served overseas, 16,640 were killed or died of wounds, 41,317 wounded and 530 taken prisoner. This total of nearly 58,500 casualties is over 50% of those who served overseas. On ANZAC Day – 25th April – every year there is a wreath laying ceremony at the memorial.

Leaving the park turn right and follow the road into Messines itself. When it joins the main road, follow round to the church, which is visible ahead of you.

Messines (now Mesen) church, St Nicholas, was rebuilt in 1928 on similar lines to the original that was destroyed during the war. The church is usually open and guided tours are available from Albert Ghekiere, who lives opposite at 2 rue de l'eglise (Tel: 057.44.40.51). An enthusiastic character, who speaks superb English, Albert has been helping visitors to Messines for a long time. For nearly twenty years he has worked on a project to replace the church bells with 'peace bells' of which there are now thirty-seven, one of them sponsored by the Western Front Association. The crypt where Adolf Hitler sheltered from a British bombardment in 1914 is also visited as part of the tour and has recently been restored. The main square is reached by following a side street from the church (rue de l'eglise). On the green in front of the town hall are several plaques commemorating the ANZACs, and the barrel of a German field gun. In the town hall itself is a very good private museum, and it is necessary to contact Albert to view it. Postcards and information leaflets are available there.

From the town hall steps go right up to the main road and here turn right, in the direction of Ypres. At the next cross-roads turn left at the CWGC sign down Nieuwkerkestraat and follow to the cemetery on the left.

A New Zealand ration party at Messines, June 1917.

Messines in 1914.

MESSINES RIDGE BRITISH CEMETERY & MESSINES RIDGE (NEW ZEALAND) MEMORIAL

The entrance to the cemetery brings you first to the New Zealand Memorial which commemorates 840 men from the NZ Division who fell near Messines in 1917-18. Like most memorials to the missing the names are listed by unit and then rank. Among them is one of the oldest NZEF soldiers to die in the war: Private L.G.Chevalier who was killed with the 2nd Otago Regiment on 7th June 1917, aged fifty-six. Private H.G.Hood was an Englishman who had emigrated to Canada, joined the CEF in 1914 and was discharged due to wounds. He went to New Zealand for health reasons, but joined the NZEF and died serving with the 2nd Auckland Regiment on 7th June 1917.

The cemetery was constructed after the war when all the graves were brought in from an area between Messines and Wytschaete. Burials total: 986 British, 332 Australian, 115 New Zealand, fifty-six South African, one Canadian and one whose unit is not known. Of these 954 are unknown; almost two thirds of the total. Many of the graves are soldiers who died in the Messines fighting in June 1917, although an earlier casualty is Lieutenant P.F.Payne-Gallwey (II-F-8). Stationed in India on the outbreak of war, he was posted from the 21st Lancers on attachment to the 9th Lancers with whom he was killed at Messines on 30th October 1914.

Leave the cemetery and take a minor road, Kruisstraat, almost directly opposite. Follow this for a while, then past a farm on the left, and just before a left-hand bend, stop.

To your left, in the distance, are the buildings of Ontario Farm. Another strong point in the German lines, it was also selected as a target for one of the Messines mines. 171st Tunnelling Company blew a charge of 60,000 lbs here on 7th June 1917. It was the only one not to produce a crater; instead there was a circular pulpy patch where the ground bubbled for several days afterwards. It was captured by units of the 25th Division.

Continue along the road, going straight across at the first cross-roads and then stop at the second.

This area was known as Kruisstraat on British maps and was part of the German defences. Major Cropper's 250th Tunnelling Company blew three 30,000 lb mines here on 7th June, enabling the men of the 36th (Ulster) Division to advance. Some years ago one of the mine craters was filled in, but the other two remain and can be reached by taking a detour down the road to the left; they are in the field to the right of this road.

Otherwise continue straight on at this cross-roads and follow the road past a farm to a scrub area on the right, at a bend in the road; Spanbroekmolen.

An aerial view of the trenches between Ontario Farm, and Messines.

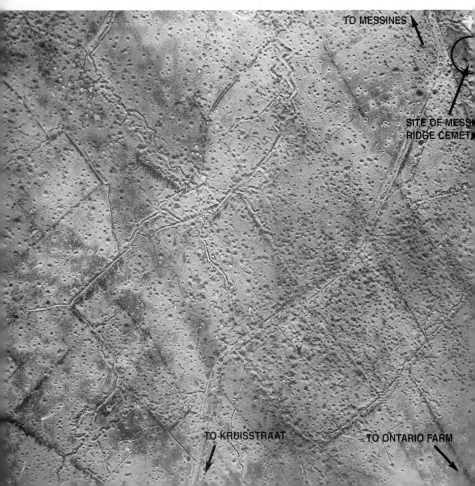

Spanbroekmolen was one of the highest German front line positions on the Messines Ridge. 'Molen' is the Flemish for windmill, and one stood on this spot before the war. The Germans created a particularly strong defensive position around the ruins of the mill, with deep trenches, dugouts, machine-gun and trench mortar positions, and even a sunken light railway, built on wooden rails to disguise the noise. It supplied the forward trenches with ammunition and bombs, and could be used to evacuate the wounded. The British lines opposite Spanbroekmolen bore no comparison, and were typical of many along the Messines Ridge. One battalion, 1/5th Leicestershires, who was in this sector in April 1915, left a good impression of the positions here (see also map).

> *Our first sector of trenches consisted of two disconnected lengths of line, called trenches 14 and 15, behind each of which a few shelters, which were neither organised for defence nor even splinter-proof, known as 14S and 15S... On the left some 150 yards from the front line a little circular sandbag keep, about 40 yards in diameter and known as SP1, formed a Company Headquarters and fortified post, while a series of holes covered by sheets of iron and called E4 dugouts provided some more accommodation – of a very inferior order, since the slightest movement by day drew fire from the sniper's posts on 'Hill 76'. As this hill, Spanbroekmolen on the map...was held by the Boche, our trenches which were on its slopes were overlooked, and we had to be most careful not to expose ourselves anywhere near the front line, for to do so meant immediate death at the hands of his snipers... To add to our difficulties our trench parapets, which owing to the wet were entirely above ground, were composed only of sandbags, and were in many places not bullet proof.*

By the time the 36th (Ulster) Division arrived in this sector before the Battle of Messines in 1917, little had changed. Major Cropper's 250th Tunnelling Company were by then preparing a huge mine to knock out Spanbroekmolen with 91,000 lbs of Ammonal. For the attack on 7th June, Zero Hour was set for 3 10am – also the time the mine would detonate. The infantry were told that to avoid any loss of momentum, if the mine did not explode at exactly that time, they were to advance anyway. On the day the mine was fifteen seconds late and by that time many men of the 8th Bn Royal Irish Rifles were already part way across No Man's Land. The debris tumbled down on to the attackers, killing and wounding a large number of them. However, the charge had

The trenches at Spanbroekmolen. (PRO)

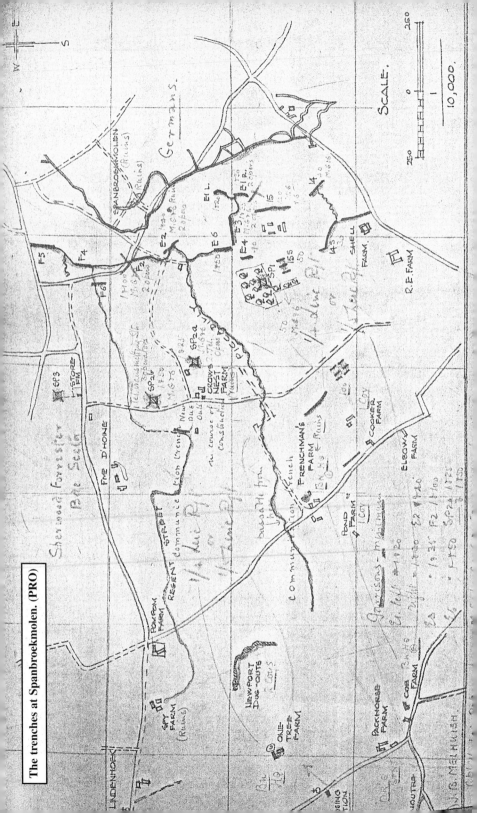

German Front Line

ROAD

TRENCH RAILWAY

SUPPORT LINE

N

An aerial view of the Spanbroekmolen position in mid-1916.

wiped out the main position at Spanbroekmolen and left a huge crater. The remaining garrison offered little resistance to the Irishmen, who were able to capture the position quite easily and move on to Wytschaete and the Messines Ridge itself. Today Spanbroekmolen is owned by Toc-H, now preserved as a memorial to all those who died here in 1917 and known as The Pool of Peace. The crater is large, the flooded part alone being twenty-seven metres deep. In the scrub to the rear of the crater are the remains of a concrete pillbox.

From the crater retrace your steps slightly, back towards Kruisstraat. A CWGC sign to the cemetery is seen on the right. Go through the gate and across the fields, which can be muddy in wet weather, to the cemetery – reached by another gate.

LONE TREE CEMETERY

The cemetery was started by units of the 36th (Ulster) Division after the Battle of Messines, when they buried their dead who had fallen in the advance here; among them, no doubt, some of the men who had died when the Spanbroekmolen mine went off late. Other graves were added afterwards, as the fighting moved on to beyond Wytschaete. Of the eighty-eight burials, sixty are men from the Royal Irish Rifles, giving it very much a 'comrades' feel.

Return to the road and turn left, passing the mine crater. Further on take a minor road on the left, Spanbroekmolenstraat, and follow it round to the right past some houses. Continue to a lone farm, known as Crow's Nest Farm on trench maps. The track now continues to the left, just past the farm, where it becomes a bridleway, getting narrow and bordered with small trees and a fence. Follow to its conclusion where it meets a minor road. Turn left, and at the T-junction turn right taking the road into Wulverghem. This road comes out with the churchyard on your right. At the main road go straight across, and follow this route back to St Quentin Cabaret Cemetery and your vehicle.

1. 1st Bn Canadian Infantry *War Diary* 13.10.15, PRO WO95/3760.
2. Bairnsfather, B. *Bullets and Billets* (Grant Richards Ltd 1916) p.222-225.
3. Hills, J.D. *The Fifth Leicestershire: A Record of the 1/5th Battalion the Leicestershire Regiment TF during the War 1914-1919* (Echo Press 1919) p.25.
4. For further information see MacDonald, L. *They Called It Passchendaele* (Michel Joseph 1978) p.46-47.

Chapter Twelve

'PLUGSTREET WOOD' WALK

STARTING POINT: **Hyde Park Corner (Royal Berks) Cemetery.**
DURATION: **4½ hours.**

WALK SUMMARY: *A comprehensive walk around the 'Plugstreet Wood' area, visiting all the military cemeteries, going into the wood itself, and following quiet roads and tracks. It is therefore suitable for walkers of all abilities.*

Park your vehicle either outside the cemetery or in a tarmac area beside a nearby café – which can provide refreshments either before or after the walk.

Ploegsteert, or 'Plugstreet' as it was known to British troops, was the southern most sector in the Ypres Salient, and close to the French border. Dominated by high ground north of the village at Hill 63 and by a huge wood, after fighting in October 1914 front lines were established east of Plugstreet Wood and trench warfare began. Being in low-lying ground, those early occupants of the area soon realised that

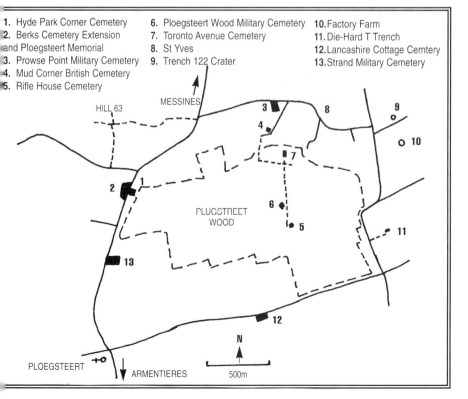

1. Hyde Park Corner Cemetery
2. Berks Cemetery Extension and Ploegsteert Memorial
3. Prowse Point Military Cemetery
4. Mud Corner British Cemetery
5. Rifle House Cemetery
6. Ploegsteert Wood Military Cemetery
7. Toronto Avenue Cemetery
8. St Yves
9. Trench 122 Crater
10. Factory Farm
11. Die-Hard T Trench
12. Lancashire Cottage Cemtery
13. Strand Military Cemetery

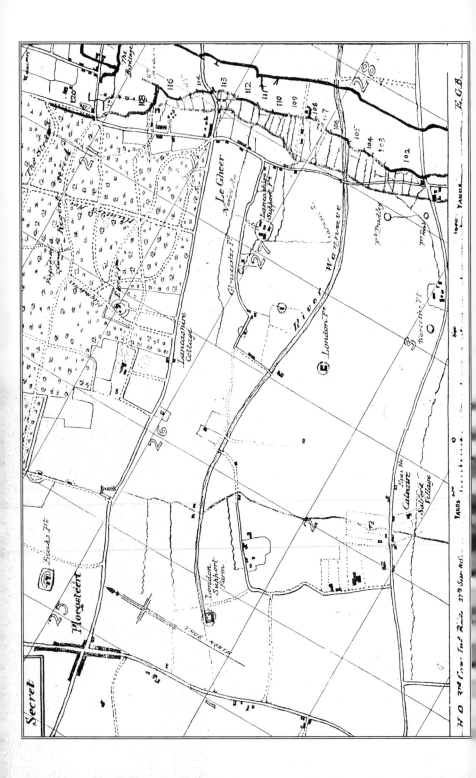

Secret

Ploegsteert

H.Q. 3rd Corps. Int. Police. 37ᵗʰ Scan-Ref.

digging here was often quite impossible and many of the 'trenches' were in fact breastworks; defence lines constructed above ground. By the close of 1914 Plugstreet Wood was held by 4th Division, and a further action took place on 19th December following which the front lines stabilised for the next three and a half years. Thereafter Plugstreet was considered a 'quiet' sector, if indeed any part of the Western Front could ever be called quiet, where divisions going to and from major battles were placed. In 1915/16 it was also used to acclimatise many New Army divisions in the business of trench warfare. Mining operations began in 1916, and two mines were blown as part of the Battle of Messines on 7th June 1917, when Australian troops pushed eastwards to La Basse Ville. During the Battle of Lys in April 1918, both Hill 63 and Plugstreet Wood fell in the German advance, being recaptured by units of the 31st Division in September 1918.

HYDE PARK CORNER (ROYAL BERKS) CEMETERY

Hyde Park Corner was a junction on the Ploegsteert road and the cemetery took its name from the 1/4th Bn Royal Berkshire Regiment who started it in April 1915 during their first tour of the front line trenches; the cemetery then remained in use until November 1917. Burials number: eighty-one British, four Germans, one Australian and one Canadian. Lieutenant R.W.Poulton Palmer (B-11) of the 1/4th Royal Berks, who fell on 4th May 1915, was a well known rugby player whose family were joint owners of the Huntley and Palmer biscuit business based in Reading. Young soldiers abound here – aside from an eighteen year old and six nineteen year olds, there are two even younger. Private F.W.Giles (B-13), 1/4th Royal Berks, was one of the first to be buried at Hyde Park Corner, killed on 28th April 1915, aged seventeen. The grave of Rifleman A.E.French (B-2) has attracted many visitors since a radio programme and booklet featuring his letters home revealed he was a mere sixteen. French died serving with the 18th Bn King's

The grave of Rifleman A.E.French.

185

Royal Rifle Corps (Arts and Crafts Bn) on 15th April 1916. As a result of public interest, the CWGC consented to add the correct age to his headstone; before nothing was shown.

Several pairs of brothers died in the Plugstreet sector – one half of a pair is here, his brother buried in Berks Cemetery Extension opposite. The son of James and Sarah Baird of Belfast, Sergeant S.Baird (C-5) was killed on 24th November 1916, aged twenty, while serving with the 2nd Bn Royal Irish Rifles. The grave of his brother, who died some months later, will be visited shortly.

Carefully cross the road to the military cemetery and memorial opposite.

BERKS CEMETERY EXTENSION

Burials did not begin until June 1916, when the cemetery was started by units of the 41st Division, newly arrived on the Western Front. It continued to be used until September 1917 by which time there were: 295 British, fifty-one Australian, forty-five New Zealand and three Canadian graves. Among them were two unknown British soldiers. The Ploegsteert Memorial was added after the war (see below), and when the cemetery at Rosenberg Chateau, on the slopes of Hill 63, could no longer be maintained due to the wishes of the Belgian landowner, the graves were moved to this cemetery in 1931. This separate plot has the following burials: 171 British, 145 Canadian, 126 Australian and thirty-five New Zealand.[1]

In the original cemetery are several interesting graves. Among them is the elder brother of Sergeant Baird,[1] Rifleman J.C.Baird (O-1) who died on 17th February 1917, aged twenty-two, while serving with the 14th Bn Royal Irish Rifles. The battalion *War Diary* records that after a British artillery shoot on the German lines on Messines Ridge, '... the enemy retaliated, a number of shells falling in the wood behind our headquarters: one hit a tree beside H.Q. cookhouse and exploded killing Privates Baird and McColl – Capt Gavin's and Capt McKee's servants respectively.'[2]

Two other brothers are also buried here – side by side. Riflemen L.Crossley (E-20) and W.Crossley (E-21) joined the 21st Bn King's Royal Rifle Corps (Yeoman's Rifles) together in 1914, crossed to France together and were killed together – possibly by the same shell – after only a few weeks front line service, on 30th June 1916. On this day 21st KRRC were in reserve billets between Creslow and Touquet Berthe Farms, and were hit by retaliatory fire after a bombardment earlier in the day.[3]

There are several graves of men involved in the mining operations east of Plugstreet Wood who died in 1916 while preparing the Messines mines; particularly noticeable are those from the 3rd Canadian and 171st Tunnelling Companies. Trench mortar batteries had their gun positions in the wood, and many of their casualties were brought here for burial. Among them was Bombardier W.G.Cooling (F-22) of Z/41 Trench Mortar Battery who was killed on 12th July 1916 when a round misfired, and prematurely detonated, as it was leaving the weapon. These divisional trench mortar units were issued with the 2-inch Trench

The original grave of Bdr W.Cooling.

Howitzer – the rounds they fired, due to their shape and design, were more commonly known as the 'Plum Pudding' or 'Toffee Apple'.

PLOEGSTEERT MEMORIAL

This memorial to the missing records 11,447 British soldiers who fell in the Plugstreet Wood area and between the River Douve and the towns of Estaires and Fournes from 1914 until the end of the war. Many of the names are men who fell in the Battle of the Lys in April 1918. Originally it was proposed that this memorial would be sited in Armentières, and be known by that name, but a suitable location could not be found and eventually it was erected here. Designed by Sir Gilbert Ledward, the Ploegsteert Memorial was unveiled by the Duke of Brabant on 7th June 1931; the anniversary of the Battle of Messines. *The Ypres Times,* the journal of the Ypres League, reported that a large crowd came to see the Duke, who had flown into Courtrai for the ceremony.

Among those commemorated here are:

TUNNELLER VC: Sapper William Hackett was a pre-war civilian miner who had worked at the Mauvers Main Colleries, Wath-upon-Dearne, near Rotherham. He enlisted on 1st November 1915, aged

Spr W.Hackett VC

forty-two, and as with many tunnellers, was in France within a month of joining up. He served with 254th Tunnelling Company RE and was awarded a posthumous Victoria Cross for bravery in Shaftesbury Avenue mine, near Givenchy in northern France. Although slightly out of the scope of this book, his VC citation nevertheless gives a good impression of life underground for these miners.

For most conspicuous bravery when entombed with four others in a gallery owing to the explosion of an enemy mine. After working for 20 hours a hole was made through fallen earth and broken timbers, and the outside party was met. Sapper Hackett helped three of the men through the hole and could easily have followed, but refused to leave the fourth who had been seriously injured, saying: 'I am a tunneller, I must look after the others first.' Meantime the hole was getting smaller, yet he still refused to leave his injured comrade. Finally the gallery collapsed, and though the rescue party worked desperately for four days the attempt to reach the two men failed. Sapper Hackett, well knowing the nature of sliding earth, the chances against him, deliberately gave his life for his comrade.[4]

SERVED AS BROWN: Leonard James Pope was one of many soldiers who served under a false name. Born in December 1896, he ran away from home in 1912, and made his way to Ireland where he joined the Royal Irish Regiment. Aged only sixteen, he produced false papers upping his age by two years and changed his name to Brown. In 1914 Leonard fought at Mons, Le Cateau and First Ypres with the 2nd Bn, and in 1915 at Neuve-Chapelle and Festubert, where he was wounded. He returned to the 2nd Bn for the Somme in 1916, transferred to the 2nd Leinsters and by 1917 had been wounded a further three times. He

188

Lieutenant L.J.Brown.

applied for a commission and became a Second Lieutenant in the 1st Bn East Surrey Regiment, serving with them in Italy and France, and in July 1918 transferred to 2nd Royal Fusiliers. A few weeks later Leonard was killed near Borre, on 19th August 1918, and buried there by his comrades – although after the war no grave could be found. By the age of only twenty-two Leonard Pope was a veteran soldier of four regiments, four wounds, and almost every major battle on the Western Front. For reasons that remain a mystery, his true surname was never revealed to the IWGC and he is recorded under the East Surrey panel as Brown.

THE WRONG MEMORIAL: In the immediate post-war years the Imperial War Graves Commission faced a vast task of compiling records of all those who had died in the war – and understandably many mistakes or omissions were made. Indeed names are still being added to the Menin Gate and Tyne Cot. Some men were also commemorated on the wrong memorial, and one of these was Thomas Henry Bowley. Bowley was a regular soldier who had joined the Border Regiment in 1893, and served in the Boer War with the 1st Battalion. By 1914 he was a Company Sergeant Major in 2nd Battalion, and when war broke out was offered a commission in the regiment that had been his home for more than twenty years. However, no vacancies for Second Lieutenants in the Border Regiment were then available and he was eventually commissioned in the Leicesters. However, he never served

2/Lt T.H.Bowley.

with that regiment or wore their badges. Keeping his Border badges, he stayed with the 2nd Bn until killed on Kruiseek Hill on 26th October 1914. Although buried in a makeshift trench with his men, Bowley's grave was lost in later fighting and as this sector of the battlefield was covered by the Menin Gate Memorial, he should have been commemorated there. But when the IWGC looked at their records he was officially listed as an officer in the 1st Bn Leicestershire Regiment, who were south of Armèntieres on the day Bowley died. With so many names to commemorate there was no time to double check the details and his name was therefore erroneously recorded here at Ploegsteert on the Leicesters' panel.

Leaving Berks Cemetery and the Ploegsteert Memorial, turn left onto the main Ypres road and continue to a junction by a café on the left. This was Hyde Park Corner. Here turn left down a secondary road. The wooded embankment of Hill 63 is then on your right. A few hundred yards further on, up on the right, is a discernible footpath going up the side of the hill. Follow it through the trees towards the crest of Hill 63 and where this path meets a track, stop.

Hill 63 was a high point south of the Messines Ridge which dominated the terrain west of Plugstreet Wood. It fell into British hands in 1914, and remained behind their lines until captured by the Germans in April 1918. It was re-taken by the 31st Division in September 1918. On the western side was Rosenberg Chateau – an Advanced Dressing Station where a military cemetery was established (see above), and on the southern slopes huge dugouts and tunnels were constructed by Australian engineers at the 'Catacombs'. To the east was La Hutte Chateau, used as a headquarters by 1st Cavalry Brigade in November 1914, but in ruins by 1915. However, due to its commanding position, there were several observation posts here and even today the view from the crest of Hill 63 is considerable.

A good account of the April 1918 period is given by Major R.T.Rees who was in the defences on Hill 63 at this time with the 8th Bn Loyal North Lancashires. Having served in Plugstreet Wood during 1916/17, Rees knew the ground well. But he soon found himself in a precarious position as Messines fell on his left flank, Armèntieres was known to have been captured on the right, and Plugstreet Wood was rapidly being infiltrated in front of his battalion. A telephone conversation to his commanding officer, telling Rees to hold at all costs, was suddenly cut short when the dugout occupied by this officer and the two other battalion commanders in the brigade, as well as their adjutants, was suddenly over-run by the Germans. Rees found himself the only senior field officer left on Hill 63. As the Germans visibly swarmed forward, Rees went to consider the situation.

> *I was standing with my Adjutant on the Messines road, and as we had no trenches to hold on to, I told him that I thought we might justifiably regard the position as untenable.*[5]

Hill 63 was captured, and Major Rees and his men forced into the Douve valley – under heavy fire from German machine-guns. Several days later Rees was wounded by a shell at Ravelsberg, losing a hand. He returned to his civilian occupation as a schoolmaster at Dulwich College.

Follow the track on Hill 63 eastwards and down the slopes to the main Ypres road. Cross and follow a minor road signposted with a large CWGC sign indicating several cemeteries. Plugstreet Wood is clearly visible to your right. Continue to the first military cemetery.

PROWSE POINT MILITARY CEMETERY

Prowse Point was a feature on British maps named after Brigadier General C.B. 'Bertie' Prowse DSO; it was one of several sites on the Western Front named after this brave and charismatic soldier. Prowse was a regular army officer, and served at Plugstreet in December 1914 as a captain in the 1st Bn Somerset Light Infantry; later he rose to command the battalion and by 1916 was brigadier general of the brigade in which 1st SLI served. Mortally wounded on the Somme on 1st July 1916, he was buried at Louvencourt. The cemetery here was started by the 2nd Bn Royal Dublin Fusiliers and 1st Bn Royal Warwickshire Regiment (both from 4th Division) in November 1914, and stayed in regular use until April 1918 – with a few graves added in the September 1918 fighting. Burials total: 159 British, forty-two New Zealand, thirteen Australian, twelve German prisoners and one Canadian. Among them is one unknown British soldier.

Bruce Bairnsfather, creator of the 'Old Bill' cartoons, was an officer in the 1st Royal Warwicks, and the cemetery contains many of their dead in Plot I. The only Canadian grave is that of Private W.Davis (I-F-14), 10th Bn Canadian Infantry, who was killed on 25th February 1915, during the unit's first tour of the trenches – indeed, he was their first combat casualty. Having only been in France for a few weeks, many Canadian battalions were on attachment to British formations at this time for instructional purposes. A small group of men from the 2nd Royal Berkshires are in Plot III, continuing that regiments connection with the Plugstreet area. Among them are Regimental Sergeant Major J.Campbell (III-A-4) and Sergeant W.A.Connor DCM (III-B-7): both killed on 15th October 1917 when shells fell on the front line positions opposite Warneton. RSM Campbell was the holder of the 1914 (Mons) Star and had been mentioned in dispatches. In addition to his DCM, Connor had been awarded the French Croix de Guerre. The New Zealand burials include several from the Maori Pioneer Battalion, amongst them an officer, Second Lieutenant A.P.Kaipara (III-A-26), who died on 4th August 1917.

Leaving the cemetery continue along the road for a short distance, then take the first right hand turning, following a metalled track down to another military cemetery.

MUD CORNER BRITISH CEMETERY

Those who walk these routes outside of the summer months will realise how apt the name Mud Corner was, and is, for this junction on the north edge of Plugstreet Wood. The cemetery was started on 7th

June 1917, the opening day of Messines, and continued in use until the end of that year. New Zealand graves dominate with fifty-three burials; in addition there are thirty-one Australians and one British soldier, who is unknown. The NZEF graves include many Gallipoli veterans, among them three older men: Private E.Breach (II-C-6) of the 2nd Wellington Regiment was fifty-four when he died on 26th July 1917; Privates D.Cowie (II-A-1) and A.McKenzie (II-A-9) of the Auckland Regiment were forty-three and forty-seven respectively when they were killed in June 1917. McKenzie had been at Gallipoli, and was a veteran of the Boer War.

Returning to the metalled track continue in the direction of the wood; it soon goes left and then later left again into the wood itself, and brings you out on the main ride through Plugstreet Wood.

This ride was known as Hunters Avenue by the British troops who served in the wood, and duckboards and corduroy tracks lined the route, easing the frequent problems of mud. All the other rides and breastworks were given similar names, often reflecting the units that passed through here. For example Strand, Charing Cross, Oxford Circus, Rotten Row, London Avenue, Fleet Street and Bunhill Row were all from when the 1/5th Bn London Regiment (London Rifle Brigade) served at Plugstreet in the winter of 1914/15. This unit was a pre-war territorial battalion raised in April 1908, whose London headquarters were in Bunhill Row – thus one of the names. Henry Williamson, in later life to achieve fame as author of *Tarka The Otter* and the fictional series of novels, *A Chronicle of Ancient Sunlight,* served with the London Rifle Brigade (LRB) in the wood at this time. The LRB were attached to regular battalions of the 4th Division and were largely employed on fatigue duties; repairing and expanding the

Soldiers of the Rifle Brigade in Plugstreet Wood, winter 1914/15.

network of defences in and around Plugstreet.

Others who knew Hunters Avenue were future Prime Minister Anthony Eden, then a young subaltern in the 21st KRRC (Yeoman's Rifles), on his first visit to the front line; and also Roland Leighton, fiancé of Vera Brittain, and immortalised in her *Testament of Youth*. Leighton spent several months in Plugstreet Wood with the 1/7th Bn Worcestershire Regiment, prior to meeting his death on the Somme in late 1915. He wrote the following poem, Villanelle, in April 1915 while in this sector.

Violets from Plug Street Wood
Sweet, I send you overseas.
(It is strange that they should be blue,
Blue, when his soaked blood was red,
For they grew around his head;
It is strange they should be blue.)

Violets from Plug Street Wood –
Think what they have meant to me –
Life and Hope and Love and You
(And did you not see them grow
Where his mangled body lay,
Hiding horror from the day;
Sweetest, it was better so.)

Violets from overseas,
To your dear, far, forgetting land
These I send in memory,
Knowing You will understand.

There are three military cemeteries along Hunter Avenue, and I suggest you walk to the farthest first and then come back, as there is sadly no through route in the wood; from here follow the ride south to the end where it meets the military cemetery.

Hunters Avenue today.

RIFLE HOUSE CEMETERY

Deep in the heart of Plugstreet Wood, this quiet and secluded cemetery was started by the 1st Bn Rifle Brigade of 4th Division in November 1914. These early graves are now in Plot IV, Rows E – J.

There are 229 British burials and one Canadian; among them two unknown soldiers. A very young soldier among the 1st Rifle Brigade casualties is Rifleman Reuben Barnett (IV-E-10), who died on 19th December 1914, aged fifteen. From Stoke Newington, he is ranked among the youngest soldiers to die at Ypres. Again continuing the Royal Berkshire Regiment connection, early officer losses from the 5th Bn are found here. They died during their first tour of the front line. The 11th Cheshires are also well represented from when they first came to Plugstreet, between November 1915 and January 1916. Ironically the unit returned to the wood in April 1918 during the Lys offensive.

Returning to Hunter Avenue go north; another cemetery is on the left.

PLOEGSTEERT WOOD MILITARY CEMETERY

The headstones in this cemetery are arranged in an irregular fashion, reflecting the layout as and when burials were made. There are four distinct regimental plots – comrade cemeteries. Plot II was the 'SLI Cemetery' containing thirty-two graves of men from Bertie Prowse's 1st Bn Somerset Light Infantry, with a further ten in Plot I: among them are five officers and a Company Sergeant Major. Nearby is the brave medical officer of the 1st SLI, Lieutenant J.R.Waddy MC (I-B-3), who survived the 1914 actions only to be killed on 17th March 1915. Plot III has sixteen men from the 1/5th Bn Gloucestershire Regiment who fell in May 1915, twelve from 8th Loyal North Lancs and twenty-eight Canadians, which once gave it the name 'Canadian Cemetery, Strand'. Plot IV is the 'Bucks Cemetery', and commemorates twenty men of the Bucks Bn Oxfordshire and Buckinghamshire Light Infantry, who died in April 1915. The cemetery remained in use between 1916-17, the last burial being from the New Zealand Division in August. Total burials are therefore: 118 British, twenty-eight Canadian, eighteen New Zealand, and one Australian. Among them are two unknowns.

Again returning to Hunter Avenue, follow it to the far end where it reaches another small cemetery.

TORONTO AVENUE CEMETERY

Despite having a Canadian name – after a trench that ran near the Moated Farm north of the wood – all seventy-eight graves are Diggers from the 9th Brigade, 3rd (Australian) Division, who were killed in the Battle of Messines, 7th – 10th June 1917. The four battalions in this brigade were all recruited in the New South Wales area. Most were killed at Factory Farm, east of Plugstreet Wood.

Leaving the cemetery turn right at the main ride junction, and follow the same route as you came in by, but in reverse, out past Mud Corner and back to Prowse Point. When the metalled track meets the minor road, turn right and follow to the first bend in the road. Stop, and look north-east.

From this position you are only a hundred yards from the site of the British front line in December 1914. Bruce Bairnsfather served here with the 1st Royal Warwicks on Christmas Day 1914, and his unit was one of many to be involved in a truce with the Germans. He later wrote,

> ...*a complete Bosche figure suddenly appeared on the parapet, and looked about itself. This complaint became infectious... This was the signal for more Bosche anatomy to be disclosed... until, in less time than it takes to tell, half a dozen or so of each of the belligerents were outside their trenches and were advancing towards each other in No Man's Land.*

> *It all felt most curious...Here they were – the actual, practical soldiers of the German Army. There was not an atom of hate on either side that day...It was just like the interval between the round in a friendly boxing match.*[6]

Continue to the next bend – this is the hamlet of St Yves, and just past it on the right was the site of the St Yves Post Office mentioned by Bairnsfather in his book, *Bullets and Billets*. It was in these buildings at St Yves that the genesis of the famous 'Old Bill' cartoons began; Bairnsfather often painting some of them on the walls. By 1918 all traces of the original hamlet had gone.

Staying on the minor road, follow it until it becomes sunken and joins another. Here turn right and then first left. Head for the group of trees a few hundred yards further up, to the left of the road.

Although this is private ground, it can often be entered. Within the trees is a large mine crater, from one of several mines used here during the Battle of Messines, 7th June 1917. On that day nineteen mines were blown from Hill 60 to Plugstreet, the largest ever man-made explosion to that date; and heard as far away as London and Dublin. This is Trench 122 crater, worked on by men of the 3rd Canadian Tunnelling Company, and a charge of 20,000 lbs of Ammonal was used. Just to the south another crater can be seen – this is Factory Farm crater and from a mine dug by the same unit. Here, on 7th June, a charge of 40,000 lbs

In 1955 one of the unused mines from the Battle of Messines exploded in a thunderstorm near Plugstreet Wood. Local villagers are shown standing in the crater. (John Giles)

of Ammonal blew a hole 228 feet across.

The craters were attacked by men of the 3rd (Australian) Division, then led by John Monash, who later rose to command the whole Australian Corps in 1918. Units of the 9th Brigade took these positions at Trench 122 and Factory Farm; their dead were buried at Toronto Avenue Cemetery in Plugstreet Wood (see above). The Australian official historian recorded.

> *The mine explosions and the tremendous barrage caused the great assault in its early stages to be easier than any in which Australians had been involved. The local German garrison... was entirely unstrung. The mines blew vast craters... and each shattered or buried beneath its heaped up rim the garrison of some 150 yards of trench.*[7]

Leaving the craters, return along the same road to a T-junction. Here turn left and follow this route along the eastern edge of the wood; later it goes to the right where a track joins it from the left. Stop.

This was the site of the Birdcage. It was in this sector that the

London Rifle Brigade spent the winter of 1914/15. Men used to the city streets of London found conditions here at that time very difficult.

> *When the Regiment moved into Ploegsteert there was a good deal of frost, and many of the men suffered from it, particularly in their feet. Immediately afterwards rain set in and continued almost without a break during the winter, which was one of the wettest for some time. No small amount of pluck was required to step into trenches which generally had two feet or more of icy cold water in them, on a dark night, knowing that boots and puttees would be soaking wet for two, three or four days.[8]*

Continue, following the road by the tree line. A couple of hundred yards past the last bend, a farm can be seen in the field to the left. Stop.

These farm buildings were on the site of what Henry Williamson knew as 'The Diehard T-trench' when he served at Plugstreet with the LRB in 1914. He recalled in his fictionalised memoirs:

> *The Diehard T-trench, of 'unsavoury reputation' as the current phrase went, was a bad, water-logged trench on the left of the battalion front. Before the October fighting, it had been a draining ditch of the arable field now part of No Man's Land. It lay parallel to, and just behind a quick-hedge bordering a lane fifty or sixty yards away from the eastern edge of the wood. Not only was it a natural drain, but as it projected into a salient in the German lines, it was enfiladed both down the stem and along*

Saturday Night Soldiers: men of the London Rifle Brigade in 1914.

A LRB Christmas card from 1914.

On sentry-go in a trench near Plugstreet Wood.

A soldier of the Essex Regiment snatches some rest in the front line at Plugstreet Wood.

Front line trench east of Plugstreet Wood occupied by the Essex Regiment.

the cross of the T. Everywhere it could be shot straight down from the various points in the opposing trench. A fixed rifle dominated one part of it; at least two snipers had two other places 'set'. [Here]... two men had been shot, one behind the other, one shorter than the other, by the same bullet, apparently, passing through the head of the first and the neck of the second.[9]

Continue. At the cross-roads, which is in the hamlet of Le Gheer, turn right and follow a better road along the southern edge of the wood for over a kilometre to a military cemetery.

German soldiers encounter similar problems to their British foe: a flooded German trench at Plugstreet in 1914.

LANCASHIRE COTTAGE CEMETERY

Named after a farm building on the opposite side of the road, the cemetery was started by the 1st Bn East Lancashire Regiment and 1st Bn Hampshire Regiment of 4th Division in November 1914. It remained in use for front line burials up to March 1916 and on a few occasions in later years. After the Germans captured the area in April 1918, they established a military cemetery of their own to the rear of this one, but these graves were removed after the war. Today Lancashire Cottage contains 229 British graves, along with twenty-three Australians, thirteen German prisoners and two Canadians. Special Memorials exist to two men, and there are three unknowns.

The original plot is dominated by 1st East Lancs, who have eighty-four graves. 1st Hampshires have fifty-six. Both battalions had been at Le Cateau, and on the Aisne, before coming to Plugstreet. 1st East Lancs buried eight of their original officers in this cemetery, among them Captain G.Clayhills DSO (I-B-7). Clayhills had been with the regiment since 1899, serving in the Boer War with a mounted infantry unit and awarded a DSO for bravery, along with two mentions in dispatches. The 1st Hampshires are dominated by the losses suffered on 19th December 1914. In Plot I are several LRB casualties, and the youngest soldier at Lancashire Cottage is Bugler M.Dudley (II-D-7) of 15th Bn Canadian Infantry (48th Highlanders), who died on 29th September 1915, aged seventeen.

Leave by the main gate and rejoin the road, turning left in the direction of Plugstreet village. It is reached after a further kilometre or so. At the main cross-roads in the centre of the village walk over to the church, behind which are several war graves.

PLOEGSTEERT CHURCHYARD

The 1st Hampshires buried their other rank casualties in Lancashire Cottage Cemetery – the officers were brought here for burial. Five of them are in this churchyard, including Major G.H.Parker (A-6) who was killed on 19th December 1914; he had been commanding the battalion since September, and was a veteran of the Boer War. Two other 1914 casualties were laid to rest here, the next burials being made by the Canadians who added a further two in 1915. One of them was Lieutenant H.B.Boggs, who was the first officer to be killed with the 7th Bn Canadian Infantry.

Return to the cross-roads. From here take the main road north, using the pavement and the cycle path, where necessary. Many new houses and other buildings have obscured the view to the wood. Further on, another military cemetery is reached on the right.

Ploegsteert village in 1914.

Shell damaged houses on the road from Ploegsteert to Messines.

STRAND MILITARY CEMETERY

The Strand was a long trench which led into Plugstreet Wood. An ADS was started near the section of the trench which ran close to the current location of the cemetery, and two soldiers who died of wounds were buried there in October 1914. No further burials were made until April 1917, when a proper military cemetery was established in what

Strand Military Cemetery.

The grave of Lieutenant D.P.Bell-Irving: the first Canadian officer to die in the Great War.

are now Plots I – VI; used until July 1917. Of the 351 graves, 232 are men from units in Monash's 3rd (Australian) Division who held this sector at that time. Plots VII – X were made after the war by concentrating graves from a wide area between Wytschaete and Arméntieres. In total there are now 725 British burials, 284 Australian, eighty-seven New Zealand, twenty-six Canadian, four German prisoners and one South African. Of these 356 are unknown and there are nineteen Special Memorials.

Of the British burials, many are regular soldiers who died in 1914. Private J.Harrington (IX-F-8) of 2nd Leinsters was killed during the Christmas Truce on 25th December 1914 in the trenches at L'Epinette. The first Canadian officer to die in the Great War was Lieutenant D.P.Bell-Irving (X-H-9) of 2nd Field Company Canadian Engineers. The Canadians had only been in France a few days at this time, and Bell-Irving was attached to a British unit when he was killed by shell fire on 26th February 1915.

Continuing along the main road, return to Hyde Park Corner (Royal Berks) Cemetery, and your vehicle.

1. For further information see Spagnoly, A. *Salient Points* (Leo Cooper 1996).
2. 14th Bn Royal Irish Rifles *War Diary*, 17.2.17, PRO WO95/2511.
3. 21st Bn King's Royal Rifle Corps *War Diary*, 30.6.16, PRO WO95/2643.
4. Anon. 'Sapper Hackett VC' in *The Ypres Times* Vol 1, No 29, October 1923, p.251.
5. Rees, R.T. *A Schoolmaster At War* (Haycock Press c.1930) p.110.
6. Bairnsfather, B. *Bullets and Billets* (Grant Richards Ltd 1916) p.91-92.
7. Bean, C.E.W. *The Australian Imperial Force in France 1917* (Angus & Robertson 1943) p.593-594.
8. Anon. *The History of the London Rifle Brigade 1859-1919* (Constable 1921) p.74-75.
9. Williamson, H. *A Fox Under My Cloak* (MacDonald & Co 1985) p.34.

Selective Index

205